REAL FAITH FOR REAL LIFE

REAL FAITH FOR REAL LIFE

LIVING THE SIX MARKS
OF DISCIPLESHIP

MICHAEL W. FOSS

Augsburg Books

MINNEAPOLIS

CONTENTS

INTRODUCTION

LIVING DISCIPLESHIP

SIX PRACTICES
FOR DISCOVERING A FAITH
THAT WORKS IN REAL LIFE

I. Practicing Our Faith

We met on a plane out of Pasco, Washington. A scientist with a Ph.D. in physics specializing in orbits and trajectories, he had been at a conference focusing on increased efforts to provide safety and security measures for nuclear power plants. Hanford is the nuclear power center in central Washington State.

I had the aisle seat, so I had stood when he indicated to me that he had the window seat. We struck up a conversation. Two strangers on an airplane.

"What brought you to the Tri-Cities?" he asked. "Business or pleasure?"

I explained that I had come to visit my father and brothers. "I grew up here and come back at least once a year," I said. "And what about you? What brings you to the Tri-Cities?" I asked.

He explained his mission for the government. He told me that he worked for the CIA, and that led to a discussion of how he moved from science to government. After half an hour, he asked me what I did for a living. When I told him that I was a Lutheran pastor, he turned from me and looked out the window. (I thought to myself, "Lost another one.") Then he turned back toward me and sighed. "I wish I could be more spiritual," he said.

And that began a remarkable hour-long conversation about faith, Jesus as the Risen One, his lapsed worship attendance, and life after death.

ᗡᖴ

In the beginning when God created the heavens and the earth. . . . Then God said, "Let us make humankind in our image, according to our likeness."
—Genesis 1:1, 26

I believe in the immortality of the soul because I have within me immortal longings.
—Helen Keller

We have been created with an inner hunger, with a need for God. To be human is to be spiritual. To be a man or woman is to have eternal longings. When we neglect this part of ourselves, we have little or no spiritual resources that we can call on to meet that deep need, to satisfy our spiritual hunger.

This book was written to help you grow deep. It was written to help you on your journey of spiritual discovery and renewal. So it's more than a book; it is workbook or notebook for the soul. Its pages will invite you to be open to hear the greatest call on earth, the call to Jesus the risen Messiah. This is the call of our deep hunger, and it puts words and content to our deepest longings.

That's what happened on that airplane. I was invited into the spiritual depths of a perfect stranger's heart. He had few words to express this inner stirring, and any spiritual practices available to meet his hunger had been discarded as useless years ago. We can only guess what circumstances led him to the discovery of his spiritual need. I have no idea what happened after our conversation. I have prayed for him and hoped to meet him again. But I don't expect to. Instead, I simply tried to introduce him to Jesus in a new way. Not unlike the disciple Philip's invitation to "come and see."

❦

The next day Jesus decided to go to Galilee. He found Philip and said to him, "Follow me." Now Philip was from Bethsaida, the city of Andrew and Peter. Philip found Nathanael and said to him, "We have found him about whom Moses in the law and also the prophets wrote, Jesus son of Joseph from Nazareth." Nathanael said to him, "Can anything good come out of Nazareth?" Philip said to him, "Come and see." When Jesus saw Nathanael coming toward him, he said of him, "Here is truly an Israelite in whom there is no deceit!"
—John 1:43-47

There are many fascinating aspects to this text. I'd like to lift up two. The first is that Philip addressed the spiritual hunger within Nathanael by inviting him to come to Jesus. And yet, Nathanael was skeptical.

How many of us display this same kind of spiritually skepticism? We participate in worship and listen to sermons, sing hymns and maybe even serve in the congregation. But our hunger has persisted. Or we don't know if we were growing spiritually. We have lost sight of the signs of growing in Christ's presence. We know others whose spiritual needs are bursting to life, but we have few resources with which to respond.

We face a culture of spiritual apathy, which is a consequence of losing our way. The first response of souls in lethargy is always skepticism. We wonder: Can I really experience something more in my spiritual life? Does Jesus really have an answer to that deep hunger I feel?

There is a way, a path that can open our spiritual journey of life to an eternal destination. There are signposts that we can pass along the way that will confirm our journey's destination. We call them *The Marks of Discipleship*. They mark the pathway of spiritual growth. We meet them again and again as they lead us through the spiraling lane of meeting our spiritual hunger and growing in God. The invitation is to begin. And then we are called to return to each practice and grow deeper in our understanding and practice of our faith. The Marks of Discipleship are spiritual aids that are biblical and have grown out of the tradition of the Christian Church. By the power of the Holy Spirit, they can help us find our way again. Our skepticism can be turned to joy, our apathy to spiritual energy, and our inability to meet the spiritual hunger in others can be changed into spiritual daring and skill.

The second remarkable aspect of the call of Nathanael that is worth noting is that Jesus recognizes him. Jesus knows him.

When we journey toward the risen Savior, we will discover that he has been calling to us, waiting for us, and loving us all along. We meet the One who truly knows us. This Knowing One understands the depths of our hunger and invites us to come and follow. When we are met by such gracious knowing, our response will be the same as Nathanael's response. In gratitude, we will fall before this One in whom we meet the forever future. At his feet, this side of Easter, our deepest spiritual hunger is satisfied, and our forever journey continues.

Our spiritual calling is not to reach a particular destination and then stop. It is an eternal invitation to grow, to become all that we are most capable of becoming. This is the promise of our creation, fulfilled only in the endless presence of the One who, in creating us, made an investment of love in this world. Our lives will never be purposive until we discover our call in God who is our creative beginning and lord of our endings. Nathanael found that meeting point between beginning and end in Jesus. At that very moment his life took on the purpose that would guide him from skepticism into the joy of complete faith commitment.

Questions for Reflection

❧ Have you ever experienced the spiritual hunger of that man on the airplane? What did it feel like? Was it met?

❧ How has your eternal longing led you to faith questions or discoveries?

❧ In what ways do you think our culture is spiritually apathetic? How does apathy fit with skepticism?

❧ How is your life like Nathanael's?

II. Joy and Happiness

I came that they may have life, and have it abundantly.
　—John 10:10

The word "joy" is too great and grand to be confused with the superficial things we call happiness. It was joy and peace which Jesus said he left [us] in his will.
　—Kirby Page

The call of Jesus to each of us is the invitation to joy, but we have often confused joy with happiness in our time. Happiness is an echo of joy, entirely limited to time and circumstance. Just as an echo is a temporary reflection of a real voice, so happiness wears the mask of joy but cannot last. Happiness is found at the amusement park. It is as easily lost as it is found. In the absence of the real voice, the real word of joy, we easily become addicted to being happy. And echoes, after all, are better than silence to the longing heart.

Joy, on the other hand, is an inner quality that can exist above and beyond time and circumstance. Joy is the inner pleasure born of purpose and achievement. As such, joy is the parent of personal significance. Joy grows over time. Joy is cumulative. So we see persons of deep joy even in the midst of circumstances that could never produce happiness. That's why Jesus could promise, "I came that they may have life, and have it abundantly" (John 10:10). And at the same time declare, "If any want to become my followers, let them deny themselves and take up their cross and follow me. For those who want to save their life will lose it, and those who lose their life for my sake will find it" (Matthew 16:24-25).

Happiness has nothing whatever to do with denying one's self. Joy is not possible without it. A deep sense of purpose cannot be cultivated in the life that is not willing and able to set itself aside. No wonder, in our age of addiction to happiness, there is so little joy. The call of God, that deep inner hunger, is all about discovering joy. That's what my fellow passenger was expressing on the plane. He was longing for joy. Just being happy was no longer sufficient.

In our own hearts, we know that this is so. When we live for happiness instead of joy, our lives are spent for things, but not life. Yet we long for life that has depth, which experiences joy rather than passing happiness. We have been created with the expectations of eternity. Addiction to happiness leads us from real life into lesser substitutes, pretenders that promise joy but give only momentary happiness or distraction.

❦

I didn't want to go to visit her, because I knew she was sick and dying. Still, in my heart I was being drawn to her home. When I walked into her room with it's makeshift hospital arrangement, she looked up, smiled, and said, "Pastor Mike, I am so glad you have come. I was hoping you would come."

We talked for a long time, and we prayed. Then, as I bent to kiss her forehead, not knowing if I would see this wonderful woman alive again, she whispered. "Did you know that when you came in you were surrounded by a white light?" And I said, "No." She smiled and said, "I've always thought of you as an angel."Then she nodded off to sleep, exhausted by the conversation.

And I knew who had called me there . . . who had entered that room with me. I left with a joy that I had not expected. This was a joy that was born of a calling beyond my own self, from outside of my own desires and will. And even in my grief for her, I still knew joy and life . . . and it was abundant.

Questions for Reflection

❧ How is joy different from happiness?

❧ Can you feel joy and be without happiness?

❧ Does it make sense that joy is only possible when we lose ourselves, live beyond our own wills and desires?

❧ How is our world addicted to happiness?

III. The Call

See what large letters I make when I am writing in my own hand! It is those who want to make a good showing in the flesh that try to compel you to be circumcised. . . . May I never boast of anything except the cross of our Lord Jesus Christ, by which the world has been crucified to me, and I to the world. For neither circumcision nor uncircumcision is anything; but a new creation is everything! . . . From now on, let no one make trouble for me; for I carry the marks of Jesus branded on my body.

—The apostle Paul, in Galatians 6:11-17

Pain is no evil, unless it conquers us.

—Charles Kingsley

Note the personal tone of Paul's writing above. These few verses are book-ended by two remarkably intimate physical reflections by Paul. The first bookend is Paul's own handwriting. We don't know why he had to print so large, except that it probably was due to a physical ailment of some sort. Paul spent the second half of his life responding to Christ's calling, in spite of the limitations caused by a physical infirmity that could have derailed it. Instead, God surrounded him with others who could write for him.

The second bookend tells us that Paul was willing to sacrifice his own body for the sake of his call. The call was worth whatever sacrifice he had to make, and he bore on his own body the signs of his passion to follow the call.

This is core. Paul's call is core. And so is ours. Not just as Christians, but as human beings. As the conversation on that plane with a stranger reveals, to be human is to have placed within the deepest part of us a longing for eternity, a longing for purpose. This is within all of us, denied or active, because God intends us to grow into forever. This is our call.

There is no real call from God without cost. The truth of the matter is that there are no "cost-free" decisions in this life. We will spend our lives for something. We will, in Paul's words, carry the marks of our choices on our bodies. The only real question is whether we will carry these marks of living for something of true value. God invites us into a life that is deeply meaningful, profoundly worthwhile. But the call of God to live into forever will not be pain free any more than any other call we follow will be without personal sacrifice and difficulty. The call is our life path. More than a destination, it invites and pulls us into the world. Another word for Christ's calling is "discipleship," and it is Jesus's invitation to true joy.

Even a quick reading of the four narratives of Jesus and his disciples, called the Gospels, makes it clear that disciples are not always happy. Disciples experience joy and sadness, hope and grief. We slide up and down the scales of real emotions, but joy is not dependent on the ups and downs of our circumstances. In our deepest selves we know that there is a grounding, a strength that sustains us. Our joy is sustainable and renewable. This joy can be measured by how we live the Marks of Discipleship that define our life journey with Christ. The Marks of Discipleship, explored more fully later, are the practices of our faith that re-ground us in our call, our hope, and our joy.

It doesn't get more deeply personal than this! Just as Paul's core, the center of his life, is his highly personal sense of call, so our callings are unique to each of us. If you want to discover your own core, think back on an occasion when you experienced true joy, an experience of happiness that was deeper than momentary pleasure. It is likely that you experienced this joy as you made a connection with a sense of purpose and worth that was far beyond the expected. It took you above and beyond. It caused you to be caught up in a moment of self-giving that returned to you so much more than you could have given. Any amount of time and energy that you gave was more than worth it.

The echoes of this memory can unlock the door to your core, your heaven-sent purpose. If you pause long enough at its doorway, if you listen carefully enough to its word, you will hear the voice and see the presence of Jesus.

Questions for Reflection

❧ How is your present life bearing the marks of a life that is worthwhile, fulfilled?

❧ Do you agree that there are really no "cost-free" decisions in life?

❧ Think of a time when you felt true joy. How did that experience point to the core of your being? How does your present life reflect that core?

❧ Would you be willing to share that experience, and what it means to you, with a trusted friend?

IV. Called to Real Life

As Jesus passed along the Sea of Galilee, he saw Simon and his brother Andrew casting a net into the sea—for they were fishermen. And Jesus said to them, "Follow me and I will make you fish for people." And immediately they left their nets and followed him.
    —Mark 1:16-18

A clean heart can see God. And we should see God in each other. This is what Jesus taught us: "Love one another. You did it to me. That small thing, you did it to me."
    —Mother Teresa

I think most of us read or hear this text from Mark's Gospel and make an unconscious translation. We think that Jesus called these men from their vocation as fishermen to a new vocation as preachers. We think in terms of jobs. This minimizes the radical nature of Christ's call to each of us. Jesus is much more interested in who we are than in what we do. The call is to that unique spark planted within each individual child of eternity. Jesus calls us to life—abundant life—and not just to a new job.

"When I was working, I loved my job," he said. "But toward the end of my career, I discovered Habitat for Humanity. I loved pounding nails and carrying lumber because I knew that my work was for others. I always loved working with my hands, but as a professional, I never got to do it in my work life. Through my work with Habitat, and now my time at our church, I have discovered my true calling—to work with my hands and build something of real value for others."

He paused in reflection and then said with a smile, "You know, life should never be defined by the work we do. Our lives ought to define our work."

The call of Jesus is to so much more than a job. Very few of us are equipped to become pastors or preachers. But all of us are called to become disciples. Discipleship is simply "follower-ship." What or whom we follow, we serve. We can only serve one of two masters—God or ourselves. The immediacy of life often tempts us to follow our own desires and urges. Once satisfied, we find that the emptiness in our hearts remains. The immediate needs of this life often push us into jobs that are less than the eternal possibilities within us. There is nothing wrong with working in a job that that doesn't ultimately satisfy our longings if the work is done for a greater good, such as providing for our families or giving a necessary service to our community. What is wrong is when we let that job, task, or career define who we are.

I believe that much of our cultural addiction to happiness has to do with allowing the externals of life to define us. What we do, what we have, and who we choose to spend time with are not evil. They are necessary extensions of the self. But they are the lesser and not the greater self for which we have been given breath and being.

Not long ago a good friend of mine died. She had battled cancer for over three years, and there were times when we actually thought she would beat it. The last few weeks of her life descended into death with a speed that left us breathless in shock. Hers was a life well lived. She was a woman of deep faith, and she had given so much to so many. When the funeral service was held, the chapel was packed, and many of us who were unable to attend sent our heartfelt condolences.

Reflecting on her life and my own mortality, I felt well up within me the kind of joy I have been describing. I remember thinking that if I died in that moment, I would face my Creator with satisfaction. It made me reflect on all that I have done and accomplished in life, and I thought of the lives of my two children as legacies that made it all worthwhile. Two other giving people were in the world in part because of my faith, love, and sacrifice.

Interesting. Neither my work nor my accomplishments— both of which are greater than I ever imagined—would define me. Those two lives were the baseline measurements of my life purpose.

That's real life. Real life is who you are . . . given in love to others. That is what my friend had discovered in retirement. Real life was more than simply doing or getting and having. Real life is soul work. Real life is the dailyness of our doing touched by God's sparkle of eternity.

That's what Jesus called those fishermen to. It wasn't to a new job. It was to an entirely new life! This is a life that has echoes of eternity in the very midst of the mundane. To follow Jesus is to discover that you are the point where heaven touches earth. What's most real is not in what you do, but in who you are. No matter where you go or what you do, there *you* are. A real faith for real life adds to that equation this eternal truth: No matter where you go or what you do, God meets you there.

In his retirement, this Christian man described above was surprised to meet God there in such a powerful new way. I suppose if we had asked him if he would meet God in his retirement he would have said yes, but that would likely have been an answer of the intellect, and not of his heart. His heart was surprised by joy when God met him and inspired a life of substance beyond earning a living.

Perhaps you have been surprised by joy. Maybe God has met you in some unexpected way, and who you are was extended beyond the capacities that you thought were yours. If so, then you know what Jesus was offering those fishermen. For them it led to spending their lives in a manner that would change the world. This is precisely what our God calls us to do. Those first disciples didn't change the world in one great deed. Instead, it was through the daily touching of lives that accumulated over time. Good rarely overcomes evil in one fell swoop. Rather, the good grows beyond that which is evil. The lesser is always overcome by the greater.

Our lives are called to the greater, to the Good. Our work contexts will change. Our relationships with others may undergo enormous emotional shifts. But the Good will always overcome these changes in our lives. And our lives will overcome and grow beyond them as well, if we hear and follow this call of Jesus. For his call is the call to love—the ultimate good.

Questions for Reflection

⚐ What does it mean to you that the call of God is to life—not to a job?

⚐ What defines you? What would you like to define you?

⚐ What legacy will you leave? Can you name it?

⚐ If you are a follower of Jesus, in what sense are you one of the points where heaven touches the earth?

⚐ How does changing the world through the daily acts of life make sense? How can you practice it?

CHAPTER 1

PRACTICING THE GOOD IN DAILY LIFE

THE MARK OF DISCIPLESHIP: DAILY PRAYER

I. The Call to Pray

Come, let us reason together, says the Lord.
  —Isaiah 1:18

Then Jesus told them a parable about their need to pray always and not to lose heart.
  —Luke 18:1

Speak to Him thou for He hears, and spirit with spirit can meet—
Closer is He than breathing, and nearer than hands and feet.
  —Alfred, Lord Tennyson

At one of our conferences a staff member was leading a workshop on prayer. Since this conference was for pastors and other congregational leaders, we had selected a room with a capacity of fifty persons. When our staff member arrived, he found the room packed with people sitting on the floor as well as standing around the edges of the room and out the door. After an introduction, he began to talk about prayer as a Mark of Discipleship. He hadn't gotten very far into his planned presentation when a man seated on the floor in the back raised his hand insistently. Stopping, the staff member called on the participant.

"Well, you are talking about prayer as if we know how to pray," he said. "I'm a pastor, and I don't know how to pray."

With that honest statement, the staff member left his notes and began again—this time at the beginning.

❧

Daily Prayer is the first Mark of Discipleship. This is the habit of our living in relationship with God in Jesus of Nazareth. Prayer is a habit because it only comes naturally as we practice it. Though prayer is natural to the soul, we stutter and stumble in approaching the throne of God and in articulating our desires and needs, hopes and dreams.

One of the most incredible truths of Christianity is that God desires a real relationship with us. This is the desire of God's heart. Christians believe that it is in the coming of Jesus as Savior that God the Creator came to us in person. We believe that our God created us in a burst of eternal love, the same love that calls us back to God. Daily prayer affirms the relationship between Creator and humanity, bringing heaven to earth in the life of the disciple of Jesus. In prayer we rediscover and claim God's love and promises for our lives. We live eternity in the here and now.

❧

Regarding prayer, Jesus takes us as we are spiritually. That is why, when it comes to prayer, he spends so much time inviting us to come to God. In fact, the Old Testament anticipates this overture of Jesus. Note how both scriptural quotes above (the invitation from God to Israel in the prophet Isaiah and Luke's interpretation of one of the more confusing parables of Jesus) become invitations to prayer.

Although Israel had abandoned God to worship idols, still God called them into relationship through conversation, through prayer.

Although Christians understand themselves as followers of Jesus, they still need encouragement to continue in prayer, so the Savior taught a parable that elevates persistence as an essential element of prayer and faith. Jesus knows that prayer is the touchstone between faith and unbelief. In the face of evidence to the contrary, persistent prayer clings to the promises of God.

How do we know the God to whom we pray? How do we pray? How can we rediscover the soul's language? These are not simple questions. Our own judgments and prejudices get in the way. All of us have had the experience of being ignored or discounted by someone whose attention we desperately sought. More than that, many of us have internalized the indictments of others, or worse, our own scathing verdicts of our unworthiness. So we tremble at the doorway to prayer. We cannot believe that the God of the universe counts us worthy enough to listen to us, let alone respond to us. So prayer must always start with our God's longing to know and love each one of us—totally apart from any worthiness on our part. Prayer always begins in grace.

When you close your eyes and think of God, when you want to put a face on God, what does God look like? Stop now and close your eyes. Ask the Holy Spirit to open your heart so that you can see the face of God that is planted there. What does your heart believe God looks like?

For some of us, God looks like a grandfather. For some, this "grandfather in a great beard" is angry. Our experience with adults as giants begins before our conscious minds can grasp it.

If the giant is an angry adult, the child within will imprint this anger on the face of God.

For others of us, God as grandfather wears the face of a benign but powerless old man. When we want absolute acceptance, we could go to him. But his power to change the world, to influence the real actors in our life, was negligible.

Some of us will be surprised to find that God wears the face of either mom or dad. And depending on our relationship with them, that face may be filled with love or be a face that terrorizes us with expectations that we can never meet.

Still others find that the face of God their heart has claimed is that of a revered coach striding the sidelines of life with a clipboard in hand and taking notes of our errors and accomplishments. When we come before the coach, the clipboard can be taken out to reveal our shortcomings. Isn't it interesting that this spiritual coach rarely greets us with only affirmations?

Perhaps worst of all are those of us who close our eyes only to see the face of an adult whose power over us was abusive. Their smiles and compliments are deceptive. Their invitations to come are, in fact, demands for us to comply with their abuse—which is, after all, what we deserve. Though we long for a loving God, powerful and abusive people in our lives and our hearts have put this ugly face on the Creator and Giver of Love.

Now, close your eyes and think of Jesus. Think of Jesus as a real man. He is gentle, but he is strong. He longs to love you, but will give you all the time you need to sort things out and, on your own, decide to come. This is a man whose depth of understanding is clear. He desires to empower you to be the child of God you already are. His anger is toward those who would abuse or terrify—especially in the name of God. His respect for you is so great that he would rather love you from afar than to manipulate you into relationship.

This is the face God chose to reveal to the world. God gave this picture so that we would feel free to come to God in prayer—to engage in honest conversation. This is the picture of God that can unlock our soul's language, so we can speak freely with the one who knows us and loves us better than we or anyone else can. This is the face of the One who stands at the doorway to prayer inviting us in.

Questions for Reflection
❧ What face do you most often place on God?

❧ Does the face of Jesus make a difference in our ability to pray freely? Why or why not?

❧ If we have been created for relationship with God, why is prayer so difficult at times?

❧ How does it feel to know that Jesus understands both our reluctance and our need to pray?

❧ Is prayer possible without an understanding of God's respectful love for us? Why or why not?

II. Stepping into the Presence Every Day

For it was you who formed my inward parts; you knit me together in my mother's womb. I praise you, for I am fearfully and wonderfully made. Wonderful are your works; That I know very well.
    —Psalm 139:13-14

If a shepherd has a hundred sheep, and one of them has gone astray, does he not leave the ninety-nine on the mountains and go in search of the one that went astray? And if he finds it, truly I tell you, he rejoices over it more than over the ninety-nine that never went astray. So it is not the will of your Father in heaven that one of these little ones be lost.
    —Matthew 18:12-14

May you live all the days of your life.
    —Jonathan Swift

You are not an accident. God has created you with purpose. Every day, God gives to each human being the very same treasure no matter what his or her circumstances might be: twenty four hours to spend in living. God offers the opportunity for you and me to participate in choosing how we shall spend this gift of life. Daily prayer opens us to God's guiding and to discovering our inner purpose. Daily prayer is a wonderful spiritual tool that becomes a way of life.

I have never forgotten how I learned to type. I had been using a typewriter for most of my work for years using what I called the "two finger hunt and peck" method. But I was now going to get my first computer and I wanted to be equipped to use it effectively. My daughter, who was graduating from high school and bound for college, also needed to become better at using the keyboard, so this forty-year-old man and his eighteen-year-old daughter went together.

I made the decision to learn to type because I wanted to make the best use of the gift of a computer. The hours spent in class and practicing on my own slowly began to form my brain-finger connections. From those error-filled typing exercises emerged a growing ability to type with fewer and fewer errors. And the better I got, the more easily I put the computer to good use. Now, I type freely and without thinking.

Daily prayer often begins like those early typing classes. Still, we can have confidence that the exercise or habit of daily prayer will enrich us because it will connect us to the God who has created us so wonderfully. The "practice" of prayer will draw us closer to the God who seeks us in love, and help us discover our deepest selves.

Daily prayer is a special time with God. We set aside the best of our time, not the leftovers. I am a "night person," so I have my daily time with Jesus at the close of the day. Others are "morning persons" or, as a friend of mine said, "I'm kind of a middle of the day and not for long time person." Whatever your personal best time, that is the time to practice daily prayer. If you are a morning person, set aside just fifteen minutes in your alert time. If you are at your best in the middle of the day, take fifteen minutes at lunch or make one of your breaks at work a time of prayer.

Daily prayer is your opportunity to connect with God, sharing the best of who you are. God is prepared to listen and wants the very best for us in every circumstance. Daily prayer ushers us consciously into the presence of the Creator who promises to be with us always.

Identify your best time. Then find a quiet place where it is unlikely you will be interrupted. Find a comfortable posture. Some of us are most comfortable sitting in a straight chair. For others, a comfortable sofa will do. I know some who actually prefer to kneel. Whatever posture, make it simple and comfortable. (This is another reason for taking our best time. If we are too comfortable, we may fall asleep unless this is our most alert time. But if you fall asleep, don't punish yourself for it. Simply find a time and place where you can remain alert the next time.)

As you prepare for your prayer time, come with an expectant heart. Expect that God will meet you, and trust that God will bless this time.

Now, begin the conversation with God as if you were speaking to a best friend. Take time to thank God for your blessings. Mention some blessings specifically. Let your heart be open in gratitude to God. You might want to move to a time of praising God for the wonder of creation, of humankind, and of the care God provides for our world.

Next, you may want to talk about yesterday's mistakes or today's shortcomings. This prayer is called confession. But we need to understand that God invites us into confession not so that we will feel bad, but so that we can learn from it and be free of it. Whenever you confess, conclude your confession by giving thanks that God's forgiving love has sought you out like that sheep gone astray and that you know heaven rejoices at the new beginning you have received by God's grace.

Take time to share with God those things that are most important to you. What do you desire or need? Tell God about it. Be honest. Then tell God that you trust him and will entrust to him all these things.

I always follow prayer about my needs and desires with prayers for others. I mention them by name and tell God my deepest hope and desire for them and their lives. This is called intercessory prayer. At the end of these intercessions, I acknowledge that my vision is not as big as God's, so I then give those I am praying for into the care of this God who loves them more than any of us can imagine.

You may find one of your heartfelt prayers returning to you throughout the day. When that happens, simply tell God about it and regive it into the Savior's care.

At the end of your daily prayer time, sit in silence. You may want to ask God if there is something you need to hear or think about. As you sit in silence, let your soul listen. Test what you hear. You can have confidence that it is God if it is a gift that opens the day or your future to you in a new way. And in this time of silence, prepare for the leading of God throughout the day (or, in my case, the next day).

I want to challenge you to a thirty-day experiment. Set aside and use this special time of daily prayer for just thirty days. Take note of what happens within you—your responses to stress, your outlook, your response to others. You may want to make a prayer list and check it to see what has happened in response to those for whom you have prayed, for those things you have asked for yourself. Understand that you will only get glimpses of what God can do. And ask God to help you see the working of God's goodwill. Then be spiritually alert.

Questions for Reflection

❧ What is your best time of the day? Can it be a time of prayer?

❧ What place will allow you to be in God's presence with few distractions and with no fear of interruption? Can you be there consistently?

❧ What are your deepest hopes for this time with God? Share them with God.

III. The Lord's Prayer

Pray then in this way: "Our Father in heaven, hallowed be your name. Your kingdom come. Your will be done, on earth as it is in heaven. Give us this day our daily bread. And forgive our debts, as we also have forgiven our debtors. And do not bring us to the time of trial, but rescue us from the evil one."

——Matthew 6:9-13

There are times in a man's life when, regardless of the attitude of the body, the soul is on its knees in prayer.

——Victor Hugo

Sometimes in worship I whisper the Lord's Prayer. I developed this practice after one particularly difficult week in ministry. A friend had been diagnosed with a life-threatening illness, and I had spent time with him, facing his fears, anger, and despair. Then a close member of my family announced her coming divorce. Once again, my soul was driven to its knees as I listened to her outpouring of hurt and betrayal. And as if that were not enough emotional distress, I had a very difficult staff meeting in which someone's response to the confusion of change was transformed into anger and then into confrontation with me. We worked it out, but by the time the week had ended, I was spiritually and emotionally exhausted.

During Saturday night worship it happened. When the time came to lead the congregation in the Lord's Prayer, without thinking, I began whispering the prayer.

It was an act of the Holy Spirit. As we prayed, I heard the voices of hundreds of worshipers. Their voices lifted my soul. It was as if the voices of Christians from the ages joined with the members of the congregation and spoke this ancient prayer—and I truly knew that I was not alone. Faith, through prayer, unites us with one another. That union can be a source of great strength and healing. It worked within me that Saturday night.

When I feel beaten up or pushed down in life, I return to the practice of whispering the Lord's Prayer in worship, and once again I hear the voices of faith, feel their power and presence, and I am lifted up.

Matthew's rendering of the Lord's Prayer is the closest to the one most Christians use throughout the world. Every day literally millions of Christians will utter this prayer in one form or another. There has never been a more revered nor repeated prayer in the history of the world. Perhaps, the next time you say the Lord's Prayer in worship you might want to whisper it. I encourage you, as you are softly saying the prayer, to listen to the voices around you. Open your heart to this sound of faith. In that moment, be open to being lifted on the crest of the wave of faith that surrounds you. Or you may want to focus on one voice and truly listen to it. Thank God for that person and his or her faithful witness in the prayer. If you know a need they might have, lift that need to God.

❧❧

Daily Prayer can also focus on this great prayer, which the Savior has taught us. The power of this prayer is that it can open us to the Savior's presence in a wonderful way as well as spiritually connect us with others in prayer.

Find a quiet place and assume a relaxed position. Take a moment of silence to collect your thoughts and be in the presence of Jesus. You may want to imagine him sitting next to you, encouraging you and loving you. Then, slowly say the Lord's Prayer through once.

After you have repeated the prayer in the form you are most comfortable with, remain in silence for a while.

Next, begin the prayer again. But this time, you will take a moment of quiet after each section or petition of the Lord's Prayer. When you do so, you will translate your thinking into praying. Your prayer can be a personal claiming of that particular phrase or extending it as an intercessory prayer for someone else.

For example, I might begin "Our Father in heaven, hallowed be thy name . . ." and continue:

"Lord Jesus, I pray for those who do not know God as Father. I pray for (a name in particular) who is struggling in their relationship with you. Send your Holy Spirit to touch them in a new way that they might know our Father's deep love for them in a special way. And I pray that I will hallow your name today. Help me, in all I say and do, to remember that my heavenly Father is the 'God who alone is God.' Hold me in your presence even when I am not aware of you."

Or I may stop at the words, "Thy will be done on earth as in heaven" and pray:

"Almighty God, I know that your will shall be done. Today, in the choices I make, the conversations I have, the opportunities I find, let my attitude and behavior be within your will for my life. As your will is always gracious toward us, help me be gracious to others—especially those with whom I have the most difficulty. You know who they are, but I mention to you _____ . In my interactions and thoughts about them and others, help me to be responsible and gracious, even in disagreement or conflict."

Each petition of the Lord's Prayer can be prayed and extended in this manner. Weave your personal hopes and desires and needs into the phrase, "Give us this day our daily bread." For this means so much more than physical food. The eyes of faith look to God to provide for all of our needs. And if you are aware of another whose needs are not being met, include in this phrase your deep desire that they might be fed. Remember the hungry and homeless, the broken and grieving, the wealthy and the poor in your praying in response to this petition.

When you have finished this form of praying the Lord's Prayer, you may want to write down your thoughts. This can be a wonderful record of how God grows you in faith by changing your own prayers. These prayers are reflections of your spiritual growth.

At the end of this book are twenty-five attributes that can help you assess your spiritual growth. You could look back on some of the prayers you have recorded and see if there has been a noticeable change in your own attitude, those things for which you pray or no longer pray, as well as those persons for whom you have prayed and what happened in their lives.

Questions for Reflection

❧ Why do you think the Lord's Prayer has been so revered and repeated? What is it about the prayer that is so powerful?

❧ Have you tried whispering the prayer in worship? What happened, if anything?

❧ What phrases in the prayer are the easiest for you to reflect upon? Which are most difficult? Why?

IV. Persistent Prayer

Ask, and it will be given you; search, and you will find; knock and the door will be opened for you. For everyone who keeps on asking receives, and everyone who keeps searching finds, and for everyone who [keeps knocking], the door will be opened.
—Matthew 7:7-8

Let us therefore approach the throne of grace with boldness, so that we may receive mercy and find grace to help in time of need.
—Hebrews 4:16

Prayer is not overcoming God's reluctance; it is laying hold of His highest willingness.
—Richard Chenevix Trench

"When I wake up in the middle of the night," my friend said with a smile, "I always ask God who or what to pray for. Then I just start praying. And I keep praying until inner peace comes. That's when I figure I've done what needed to be done; I've prayed for whatever needed to be prayed for. It turns my sleeplessness into ministry."

There are times when God lays something on our hearts that we cannot easily dismiss. At such times God requests us to begin persistent prayer. My friend had discovered God's call to persistent prayer through his faith and his physical struggle with insomnia, but persistent prayer can also come at other times of the day or night. We might be driving along on the freeway when someone's name suddenly comes into our minds. We may feel an inner urge to pray for that person. At first we might dismiss it as a random thought combined with an inner need to make purpose out of it. Sometimes that is exactly what it is! When the name and the inner insistence refuse to go away and, instead, become even more prevalent, it can be God calling on us to intercede on behalf of someone else. I have learned over the years to pay attention to such inner stirrings.

The call to persistent prayer requires spiritual attentiveness. To develop such awareness of the soul, we must learn to listen to ourselves. As we take the time to listen to ourselves, we ask if this comes from outside of our own self-consciousness or not. Is this thought, this urge to pray, born from our own anxieties or desperate desires? If so, it is more likely a call to let it go into God's care. But as we listen, if our hearts tell us that this is from outside of ourselves, then we must trust that and turn the thought into prayer. If that prayer returns to us, again and again, then we are being invited into persistent prayer.

Not long ago I prayed for the health of a little girl. Her mother had brought her to me for prayers of healing. This little girl would be doing just fine and then, beset by sudden nausea, she would throw up. She had been losing weight. She was embarrassed and frightened. We talked and prayed. I laid hands on her and entrusted her into the care of God. They left, and I turned to other things.

Throughout that entire day and the next, she would come to mind. It wasn't as if I was thinking of her or even aware of worrying about her. Instead, she would come to mind and, with the thought of her, would always come a deep need to pray again for her. When I would pray I experienced a strange sense of urgency and, with it, the need to keep lifting her up to our heavenly Father. At times I would even picture her being taken into the lap of the Savior like the little children in the Bible.

Persistent prayer has a very clear focus and with it a sense of urgent need. In my experience, this sort of urgent prayer rarely if ever comes in response to our own needs. Persistent prayer is a form of prayer that connects us to others for their sakes, not our own.

The next time you think of someone, do an internal check to see if prayer for him or her feels like a necessary response. If not, then simply let it go as one of those random thoughts we all have on occasion. But if the need for prayer accompanies your thinking of them, then begin your prayer by asking what form of prayer is needed. Are they in danger? Is it a health issue or a relationship problem or a personal challenge? Sometimes there will be no clarity. But after you lift them up to God in prayer, the urgency subsides. At other times, you will get a sense of what the issue may be. Then you can direct your prayers accordingly. If the name and need continues to come to you, then continue your praying for them.

I have had the experience of asking someone if something was going on at a particular time on a given day only to have him or her smile quizzically and ask me why. When I tell them I felt moved to pray for them, they share that there was a challenge or need at that very hour. The power of persistent prayer is that it is an exercise in faith—in trusting that God knows what needs to be done and that your response is simply to pray.

Questions for Reflection

❧ If you have experienced the sudden need to pray for someone, describe what happened. Did you pray? Why or why not?

❧ Has someone told you that they were praying for you and, although they didn't know your need, you knew what their prayers were for? Did you think it was God at work?

❧ What are the necessary elements needed to listen within yourself and to test whether God is calling you to persistent prayer?

❧ Are you open to persistent prayer? Does this make sense to you or does it seem too strange?

V. Imaging Prayer

Do not remember the former things, or consider the things of old. I am about to do a new thing; now it springs forth, do you not perceive it? I will make a way in the wilderness and rivers in the desert.
    —Isaiah 43:18-19

Be still, and know that I am God!
    —Psalm 46:10

[Jesus] woke up and rebuked the wind, and said to the sea, "Peace! Be still!" Then the wind ceased, and there was a dead calm.
    —Mark 4:39

Before we can enjoy the peace of God, we must know the God of peace.
    —Anonymous

We do not know exactly how prayer works. We only know that the One who hears our prayers has chosen to respond. We know this through faith and through experiencing a multitude of prayers over time. Through faith we see what others cannot; we experience what others tell is impossible. That is the power of prayer in the life of the disciple. Prayer opens us to the presence of God. Once our souls are open to God, then God begins to change how we see and experience the world.

In this sense, prayer is a dangerous thing. Why? Because prayer works on the one who prays. The Spirit of God meets us in our praying and touches us with love. When we pray, we cannot help but be transformed. The powerful workings of prayer have recently been confirmed by research to have a positive effect on the one who prays and the one who is prayed for.

Our task is to simply pray and trust that, just as the Savior has promised, God will take the focus of our prayers and use it as God judges is best. Imaging prayer takes these truths and creates a focus for them.

Years ago I read an article that changed how I prayed for those receiving chemotherapy for treatment of cancer. The article and author, long since forgotten, suggested that prayers that imaged the body receiving the chemotherapy toxins as healing agents would experience greater success in its treatment. The reason was that such prayer actually helped the body embrace the treatment and use it, rather than fight against the poison.

I began to meet with patients before their treatments and invite them to pray with the use of imaging. I would help them use exercises to help them relax, and then we would pray. First, we would thank God for the doctors, nurses, and technicians through whom the treatment for healing would come. Then we would acknowledge that God is the ultimate healer. Second, we would pray for the patient's body to be open to the necessary work of the chemotherapy. We would picture the body receiving a wave of helpful energy. Then, in whatever form the individual could best image that wave of energy, I would invite them to direct it against the cancer. This would often include imaging bad cells that would be killed while good, living tissue would be pictured as emerging pink and healthy. At other times, the individual would picture the organ itself that was diseased. Then I would encourage them to picture that organ receiving the energy of the chemotherapy and then pulsing with new life.

Although I was never a part of a scientific study, these sessions were regarded as helpful. At the least, patients often felt they had a greater sense of personal power through this prayer. In a circumstance that leaves people feeling powerless, this sense of personal power was very helpful. Many of those with whom I prayed would use the imaging prayer on their own at home or in the hospital.

Imaging prayer can also happen as a daily activity, providing an inner picture that brings peace and focus to our spiritual lives. In this sense, imaging prayer is a lot like meditation, the benefits of which have recently been shown through a variety of Harvard University studies. Imaging prayer is one form of Christian meditation.

To practice imaging prayer, find a quiet place and get into a comfortable position. Take three deep breaths, each time holding them and then exhaling to the count of six by breathing through your mouth as if you were blowing a candle out with a sustained breath.

Next, picture in your mind a favorite place—a place you associate with peace and safety. (Often people will choose a cabin in the woods or a chapel. Others will imagine themselves in a favorite room or a field of flowers.) Picture the colors as vividly as you can. Note the color of the sky, the color of the grass or the water. See if you can feel the touch of the wind.

Now, picture the sun above. Feel the warmth of the sun on the top of your head. It is a gentle warmth. It is the physical sensation of God's love. Feel the love of God moving from the top of your head through your body to the soles of your feet. Bask in the wonderful warmth of God's love for you.

You may want to picture in your mind's eye the coming of Jesus across the field or over the lake's waves or entering the place you picture yourself in. As Jesus comes to you, hear him speak words of welcome and love for you. He is glad that you want to be in his presence. The point of imaging prayer is to be at peace in the presence of God. The use of mental pictures simply helps us.

An outgrowth of imaging prayer is called centering prayer. In centering prayer, you make the same preparations as those listed above. Then, set a clock (preferably one that doesn't make noise) for fifteen or twenty minutes, though you may want to start with five or ten minutes in your first attempts. Choose an attribute of God and focus on it. I have often found myself focusing on Jesus as the rock of salvation. The words, "You are my rock, O Lord" have often been a mantra I would repeat. At other times I would simply picture a great rock, like the Rock of Gibraltar, as the steadfast presence of Christ in my life. I remain focused on this aspect of the Lord through the time allotted. When my meditation is interrupted by extraneous thoughts, I simply let them go. I will neither get caught up in them nor will I feel badly because of them. Such thoughts are natural and decrease only as we practice this form of prayer.

These forms of prayer can be learned at centers where Christian spiritual direction is taught. I believe that it is important to have others who share these experiences available to help us understand some of the experiences that can occur through these forms of prayer.

But remember, imaging prayer or centering prayer is about being in the presence of the God we know in Jesus Christ. This is not a vindictive, judgmental, or abusive God. This is the God of love the Bible makes known.

Questions for Reflection

❧ Have you had the experience of imaging prayer? What happened?

❧ What would some of your special places be? Choose one on which you could focus in an imaging prayer?

❧ What attribute of God could you focus on in an exercise of centering prayer?

VI. Continuous Prayer

Rejoice always, pray without ceasing.
      —1 Thessalonians 5:16-17

Likewise the Spirit helps us in our weakness; for we do not know how to pray as we ought, but that very Spirit intercedes with sighs too deep for words. And God, who searches the heart, knows what is the mind of the Spirit, because the Spirit intercedes for the saints according to the will of God.
      —Romans 8:26-27

O Lord, thou knowest how busy I must be this day. If I forget thee, do not thou forget me.
      —Lord Ashley, before the Battle of Edge Hill

Continuous prayer is a way of living in the presence of God. I love the Lord Ashley prayer. It reminds us that we are in the presence of God even when we are not consciously aware of it. The presence of God is like the air we breathe. How often are we aware that we are breathing? Isn't it true that we are most aware of it when we are forced to turn our attention to it through circumstances? A runner's awareness of her breathing allows her to pace herself or use energy in an efficient way. On the other hand, an asthmatic becomes acutely aware of his breathing when his airways are suddenly constricted. So it is with God's presence. We are most aware of God's presence when we consciously focus on it through need or exercise of will. Yet even when we aren't focused in this way, God is still there.

The practice of continuous prayer is based upon this simple awareness: whether I am conscious of God's presence or not,

God is always near. So whatever I do can be done, not only in his presence but as a prayer.

I have been an avid runner for nearly thirty years. In fact, I can estimate that I have conservatively run more than fifty thousand miles in that time. But one of the great joys of running for me is that I can turn it into prayer. When I am running and it is pushing me, either through difficulty in breathing or muscle responses, I think of someone I know who cannot run. Then I pray, "Lord, let each step I take be a prayer for them. I will keep running as a prayer, because I know they cannot run."

The practice of continuous prayer allows me to start talking to God at any time—with my eyes open or closed. Of course, I strongly recommend keeping your eyes open when you are praying while driving! And rather than remain angry at someone who has just cut me off on the freeway, I will often pray that they make it safely to wherever they seem to be in such a hurry to get to, and I pray that those around them be safe too!

Continuous prayer is much more than "prayer on the run." Continuous prayer is an outgrowth of daily times of prayer. We move in and out of our conscious awareness of God's presence as easily as good friends can pick up a conversation after a lapse of time. Continuous prayer recognizes God's willingness to hear, God's desire to love us and be loved in return, and our confidence in the consistency of Christ's goodwill for our lives.

There is no activity that is healthy and good that cannot be translated into a form of continuous prayer. The teacher can make teaching a prayer for her students. A police officer can take his or her duties and transform them into a prayer for a peaceful society. A mechanic can take her work and make of it a prayer for the safety of those who depend on the vehicle she is fixing.

Recently a friend of mine shared how he takes faith into his work as a professional psychologist. He will simply ask at an appropriate time, "How does your faith help you in this?" If the answer indicates the individual chooses not to discuss faith matters, then they move on in the session. But most of the time, there is an eagerness to bring faith to bear on the issues at hand. And with that comes an opportunity to bring prayer into the mental health needs of the individual or couple.

After nearly twenty-five years in ministry, I decided that I no longer wanted to simply *tell* people I would pray for them. At what seems an appropriate time, I will simply stop what I am doing and pray with that person then and there. This means that phone conversations—many of them long distance—have become occasions for prayer! Continuous prayer understands that God is always available to us.

Not long ago, a speaker at a conference I attended shared her struggle with a life-threatening illness. She had beaten it once, but it had returned. She shared that her peace comes whenever she begins to despair or feel anxious. She simply repeats the mantra, "God is on the job." That is to say, "No matter how I feel or what I fear, God is still God." What a marvelous form of continuous prayer!

Turning our deepest feelings, tears, and anxieties into prayers is a very effective expression of continuous prayer. When I entered the house, I could feel the grief. Their eighteen-year-old son had been driving his truck and, somehow, ended up hitting another vehicle in the intersection. He had flown through the front windshield and died instantly. The grief of this mother and father was palpable. I remember seeing the utter fatigue on his mother's face. And there was a moment when she looked at me and said, "Pastor, I can't even pray. Every time I pray, I just get caught in all of what I feel and no words come. Am I losing my faith?"

"No," I said. "Instead, the Holy Spirit is taking those overwhelming feelings and making a prayer out of them. I don't know if there are human words that are adequate to express what you are feeling. But God knows, and God hears the ache of your heart."

That is what Paul tells us in Romans 8:26-27. When we understand the loving heart of God in Jesus Christ, we know that the Spirit of God exercises continuous prayers that take the form of feelings that we cannot even articulate. How many times haven't we known what to pray for—or even how to pray—in a difficult situation? Continual prayer clings to the presence of God, knowing it is enough. By faith we can claim what the grieving woman came to know in her heart when she read and trusted the words of Paul. She knew that prayer consisted of much more than words.

❦

How can we practice or grow continuous prayer in our lives? There is a three-step process that can help.

❧ First, take time at the beginning of the day to give the day and all of its activities in advance to God. Tell the Savior that you will trust him with each situation and every interaction of the day.

❧ Second, during the day, remind yourself that you have asked Jesus to walk with you through the day, that his presence is with you no matter what.

❧ Third, whenever appropriate, take a moment to begin or continue your conversation with the Savior over what is happening or what has happened. Thank him for keeping his promise to be with you. Then, look back on the hours that have passed and see if you can catch a glimpse of his touch to you or through you in the life of another. See if the Spirit has opened your mind to new ways of thought or new alternatives for problem solving. And if you see any of these things, thank God for them.

In this way, continuous prayer will be like a clear stream of living water that will run through your day. You will have times to be refreshed by it. There will be times when your spiritual thirst will be satisfied in it. But whether you are consciously aware of that stream or not, it still flows.

❧❧

There are so many ways that we can experience prayer in our daily walk as a follower of Christ. These have been just a few suggestions to encourage regular times with God and to provide alternatives for your spiritual growth. Not all of the suggestions will fit you. Some will become meaningful only over time. It doesn't matter. What matters is time—time for you to grow in your knowledge and trust in the loving God we meet in Jesus of Nazareth; time for God to touch your life and help you grow deeper in faith; time to be connected to the eternal will of God.

Questions for Reflection
❧ How often do you think of praying during the day? How could you develop a stronger sense of continuous prayer in your life?

❧ How would you feel about publicly praying for someone as a need arises?

❧ Consider developing your prayer "pattern." Would the pattern be at regular times or hours? Before certain activities?

CHAPTER 2

OUR HABIT
OF WEEKLY RENEWAL

THE MARK OF DISCIPLESHIP:
WEEKLY WORSHIP

I. The Gift of Sabbath

*So God blessed the seventh day and hallowed it, because on it God rested
from all the work that he had done in creation.*
 —Genesis 2:3

*The hour is coming, and is now here, when the true worshipers will wor-
ship the Father in spirit and truth, for the Father seeks such as these to
worship him. God is spirit, and those who worship him must worship in
spirit and truth.*
 —John 4:23-24

Worship is transcendent wonder.
 —Thomas Carlyle

The nature of God is a circle whose center is everywhere and whose circumference is nowhere.
    —St. Augustine

My illness had persisted, its symptoms sporadic, for over eight months. The diagnosis was illusive. It was a short list of possibilities—most of them carrying tragic, life-changing consequences for my young family and me. I began to wonder if congregational ministry would be possible. There were times when, without warning, the room would spin and the resulting wave of nausea would leave me hanging on the altar for support. And I wondered where God was in all of this.

One Sunday, after my colleague had given the sermon, I stood to begin the liturgy of the Lord's Supper. That's when it happened. Welling up within me was a feeling of gratitude so profound, so remarkable that I felt blessed. It was a touch of God, and I knew that worship was not about what I could do or how well I could do it. Worship is about the coming of God. In the midst of the Scripture reading, the preaching, and singing God shows up. In worship, people who long to connect with the Spirit can heal their heart's hunger. In that remarkable moment I knew that I would be made well. Two months later a diagnosis was made, and treatment led to my healing.

❧

When God hallowed the Sabbath, there was so much more going on than an eternal affirmation of our need for rest or balance in life. Many see the creation of humankind as the apex of God's creative work in Genesis 1. But I wonder. Is it possible that the pinnacle of that first creation account is in the making of Sabbath? In creating the Sabbath, God set aside a time for rest and for worship, a time for humankind to recognize its relationship to the

Creator and all created things. Worship was not an afterthought of the Creator but affirmed what is essential in human beings.

The debate over how humankind differs from the apes or other mammals has focused on intelligence. Given the discovery of a higher IQ in animals as well as the seemingly prevalent consequences of our collective intelligence, this measurement for differentiation has been discarded. We are not superior to the animals by virtue of our intelligence or its use.

What finally separates humanity from the animal kingdom is simply this: We are not aware of any animals that worship. No human civilization has ever emerged that did not, in one form or another, worship. The universality of worship speaks to the inner purpose planted within us. Our longing for eternity draws us to worship. And the best of worship brings us into the presence of the One who created Sabbath for us.

Jesus has said, "The Sabbath was made for humankind, and not humankind for the Sabbath" (Mark 2:27).

Worship is God's gift to the human soul. The soul's thirst to know God is sated in worship. God is present when hymns or songs of praise are sung, when prayers are said, when the Scriptures are read, and when the sacraments are celebrated. In worship, which is less about what we do or how we do it and more about the One in whom we gather, the longing of our souls is touched by forever.

"Pastor Mike, will you lead us in prayer?" asked Jeff, our Saturday night worship leader. He had gathered the musicians and vocalists together for a prayer before the service began. He looked at me and asked me to lead. I was more than happy to pray with them, saying:

"Lord Jesus, thank you for the privilege of leading worship tonight. Thank you for the gifts that make it possible for us to lead, and thank you for this team and their willingness to serve you through worship. Now we ask that you take this time and, by the power of your Holy Spirit, make of it what you alone can create—true worship. Help us do the best we can so that we can get out of the way for you. Touch all who come. Meet them, we pray, in this worship. In your name we pray, Amen."

❧

Worship requires excellence, because the God we worship in Jesus Christ is worthy of our best . . . and not because our excellence makes God's coming possible. In fact, leaders are to do their best precisely so that we can get out of the way in order to prepare the way, for the coming of the Lord.

The sacred meeting time called worship happens when God's Sabbath gift to us meets our reverence, and praise is our response to this giver and gift. The human soul that does not worship shrinks into itself. That which was created to house eternity, that part of us that longs to be embraced by forever, shrinks to the confines of its own desires. All we need do is imagine those cultures that have forbidden worship to see how they have sunk into the ugliness of selfishness—with all of its consequent greed and tyranny.

Worship is essential to the beauty and life of the soul. Sabbath is God's wonderful affirmation of the best of being human—not what is perfect, but what is best. The best within us is awakened in this presence. Few people feel as fully alive as those who have truly worshiped.

So weekly worship is the second practice of discipleship. This Mark of Discipleship is an invitation to meet God . . . and the best in ourselves.

Questions for Reflection

❧ What does it mean for you to "meet" God in worship?

❧ How does the sabbath complete God's creation?

❧ What do you think of the idea that humanity differs from the animals not primarily by intelligence but by worship?

❧ How does worship bring out the "best" in us?

II. Our Soul's Renewal

O come, let us worship and bow down, let us kneel before the Lord, our Maker! For he is our God, and we are the people of his pasture, and the sheep of his hand.

—Psalm 95:6-7

When [Jesus] came to Nazareth, where he had been brought up, he went to the synagogue on the sabbath day, as was his custom.

—Luke 4:16

The universe is centered on neither the earth nor the sun. It is centered on God.

—Alfred Noyes

"Does this mean I have to sell my cabin at the lake?" he asked incredulously.

I was talking with a board member about the Marks of Discipleship. When we came to weekly worship, he had this question. For him, the lake cabin was a place for family and restoration. Was weekly worship at Prince of Peace going to require the sale of this wonderful place?

"No," I replied. "My assumption is that just because you are at the lake doesn't mean that your need to worship goes away. Maybe you could have a time for family worship. Or is there a church nearby that you might attend while you are at the lake?"

He smiled. "Well, there is a small Methodist church just down the road. We've often thought that we would like to worship there."

❦

Christians believe that when Jesus came to earth he became fully human—with all the needs that come with becoming a man. So it is natural that he would worship in the synagogue on the Sabbath, as Luke records, "as was his custom." The need to worship was just as deeply placed within Jesus as it is in you and me. The desire for living beyond ourselves, living for a purpose, is the source of our need to worship.

Without worship, we confuse the temporary satisfactions of pleasure for the eternal joy of God's gift of purpose for our lives. And our soul begins to shrink. In our culture, we have talked ourselves into the idea that weekly worship is optional. Unfortunately, the Bible tells us something very different. Worship is essential. To be truly, fully human is to worship—regularly.

When you go to worship, what do you expect? For some of us, the answer is probably "nothing." We have become so accustomed to a particular form of worship, with its predictable sequence and language that the best we can hope for is more of the same. This can provide a sense of security in a changing world, but it may have nothing to do with renewing the spirit.

What do you expect in worship? Do you come expecting to meet God? Do you prepare to be touched, healed, and changed by the love of this God who alone is God? The truth is that what we expect is usually exactly what we get. What would happen if, this week in worship, you came fully expecting, looking for the coming of the Savior to you? Imagine the power of meeting God in the heart's kneeling reverence. The world would change because God has changed us. We can think of some of those who have changed our world—and their habit of worship: Dr. Martin Luther King Jr., Dietrich Bonhoeffer, and Mother Teresa, to name a few. Worship was not incidental to their transformed and transforming lives.

We do not have to have the same impact on the world as these have. We need only expect to meet God, have our souls renewed and, thereby, change that little corner of the world in which we live. Such change is only possible as our souls are filled with the presence of the Almighty God. No quiet pause in the wilderness will do it; no momentary gratitude of the heart; nor personal acknowledgement of Jesus as Lord will do it. Worship is God's gift to renew our souls, to meet our need for life at its deepest.

I want to challenge you to worship weekly for just three months. Go with high expectations. Go seeking God. Let your soul watch for the coming of the Savior. Open your heart and mind to the gift of worship and see what happens.

Questions for Reflection

❧ How has worship been a gift to you?

❧ Do you expect to meet God in worship? Why or why not?

❧ What might get in the way of expecting to meet God in weekly worship?

❧ What is the connection between regular personal worship and lives that have changed the world for good? Describe someone who seems to have this connection.

❧ What good do you think God could do in the world through you? How is weekly worship a part of that great purpose?

III. Honoring God in Worship

Jesus said to him, "Away with you, Satan! for it is written, 'Worship the Lord your God, and serve only him.'" Then the devil left him.
  —Matthew 4:10

And let us consider how to provoke one another to love and good deeds, not neglecting to meet together, as is the habit of some, but encouraging one another.
  —Hebrews 10:24-25

Faith is not belief without proof, but trust without reservations.
  —Elton Trueblood

The dearest idol I have known,
Whate'er that idol be;
Help me to tear it from thy Throne,
And worship only Thee.
  —William Cowper

"I find that I can worship God best when I am out in the woods hunting or fishing," he said. "I don't need to go to church."

"I love the out of doors as much as you do," I replied. "But just worshiping God out here isn't enough. For example, which God do you worship?" I asked. "Is it the God of the beauty of the dawn and the wonder of the deer feasting in the meadow? Or is it the God who allows the rabbit to be torn apart by the fox, the God of the life-threatening storm? And how do you know that the god in your mind is really God?"

"I hadn't thought of that," he simply replied.

If worship is God's gift to us to satisfy the hunger in the human soul, then there is an eternal purpose to worshiping with others in church. In fact, the Bible tells us that we honor God when we worship God in the company of the saints. In the Bible, there is no calling to any individual that doesn't lead that person into community.

Christian faith is deeply personal, but never private. We honor God when we worship with others in church. From the beginning of time, God has sought a people to worship him. The call of God to Abraham and Sarah was also a call to their descendants. God called the Hebrew people out of bondage in Egypt and created the twelve tribes of Israel as God's holy people. Jesus first gave a new covenant to twelve men and a company of women. In one of the greatest of biblical passages that blurs the line between this time and that dimension of reality we call eternity, the author of the book of Hebrews writes: "Therefore, since we are surrounded by so great a cloud of witnesses, let us also lay aside every weight and the sin that clings so closely, and let us run with perseverance the race that is set before us, looking to Jesus, the pioneer and perfector of our faith" (Hebrews 12:1-2).

Worship is our invitation to come into a time and place where heaven and earth touch. When we pray, receive the bread and wine, hear God's word, or sing our songs of praise, we enter into a timeless community and are surrounded by those who have gone before us and those who are yet to come to faith. God is honored in a people whose destiny is beyond time and space. Whenever and wherever we worship we come into the presence of the one true God.

In the Company of Eternity

The worship space was darkened. More than three hundred candles remained unlit. The holiday season had come. Thanksgiving had already been celebrated, but Christmas was yet to come. We had gathered on this night to remember those who had died

—loved ones and friends. As each candle was lit, a name was read.

Then my mother's name was read: Adelaide Foss. The tears flowed from my eyes. As I remembered her, I thought that she had come near. This was not only a remembering, this was a celebration. My mother was in the company of eternity. Though she had died in this world, she had been reborn to new life and now transcended this time and space. She was among those who surrounded me, supported me, and cheered me.

I looked at the light that was beginning to illumine the darkened sanctuary. I could imagine an eternal sanctuary where the light came from the lives of those who could now praise God in God's presence. Their lives, like these candles, were lights of witness and honor to God. "Now," I thought, "now I am ready for Christmas."

Worship is a foretaste of new life with Christ. We gather in community not only with fellow worshipers but also with the saints who have gone before us. It is in this company of saints, both present and past that true worship happens.

Honoring God in Worship

I would propose a three-step process for honoring God in our worship:

❧ First, enter the worship space, take your seat, and, when all the greetings of those around you have ended, take a moment of silence and pray, "Lord, I come to honor you in worship today. I ask that all the things of this week that can crowd you out of my heart be set aside by the power of your Holy Spirit. Open my heart and mind to meet you and receive you today."

❧ Second, think of those whose lives have provided a faithful witness to you. Perhaps you can look around you and see some in worship with you. Then simply pray, "Gracious Father, I do not come to honor you alone. Thank you for those with whom I worship you today—both here and in eternity. Especially

I remember before you _____." You may even be able to imagine them beside you in church. Simply trust that God has brought you to this place, and the blessing of their faith surrounds you.

❧ Third, take time to thank God for all that you have received. Thank God for the relationships you have been blessed with; the guidance you may have received at just the right time; the opportunities you may have found; and the support, healing, and love you knew when you needed it the most. Take a moment to reflect on how God can take away our sin and provide a new beginning. Thank God that the promised forgiveness of Jesus is yours.

Questions for Reflection

❧ How can corporate worship be an opportunity to know God more deeply?

❧ Have you ever experienced in worship a sense of being surrounded by those who have gone before us, as a time and place where heaven and earth touch? What happened?

❧ How does worship as honoring God change how you approach worship? How do you honor God in worship?

IV. Worship As Witness

A poor widow came and put in two small copper coins, which are worth a penny. Then he called his disciples and said to them, "Truly I tell you, this poor widow has put in more than all those who are contributing to the treasury. For all of them have contributed out of their abundance; but she out of her poverty has put in everything she had, all she had to live on."
—Mark 12:42-44

For if a person with gold rings and in fine clothes comes into your assembly, and if a poor person in dirty clothes also comes in, and if you take

notice of the one wearing the fine clothes and say, "Have a seat here, please," while to the one who is poor you say, "Stand there," or, "Sit at my feet," have you not made distinctions among yourselves . . . ?
    —James 2:2-4

To worship the Holy Trinity is an art taught by the Holy Spirit. He uses various schools: the school of suffering, the school of experience, the school of knowledge. He uses people to teach this art, and one of them is you.
    —Martin Luther King Jr.

Every weekend I watch for them. They are the "walking miracles" I see each week in worship. There is the man who, after weeks in the intensive care unit of a hospital, surprised everyone by healing and returning to his home. He said it was the prayers of the church that saved his life, a claim that the medical personnel agreed with. His first act outside his home was to hobble, the very next weekend, on the arm of his wife down the center aisle of the church. He came to thank God and celebrate the gift of life again. And I watch him come back week after week.

Then there is the young woman whose marriage has collapsed and, even after her fervent prayers for a restoration of her relationship to her husband were left unanswered, she still comes to worship God and place her trust in Jesus, the Savior.

There are countless stories of those who keep coming. Their worship is both deeply personal and real, as well as a witness to those of us who know their stories. They come out of love for God. They come to give thanks for healing or simply for the gift of strength to see the worst things through. They come, not to make a statement, but out of genuine faith.

But a statement is made nonetheless. The widow observed in the temple was just such an example of an unsung saint. Unheralded by those in authority, the woman's faith was witnessed by One who saw the heart, and centuries of Christians have learned of her worship and been inspired by her simple act.

Honoring God in our worship witnesses to the world. When we worship, we do not worship for ourselves alone. We worship for those who, unknown to us, have a need of seeing us there. God takes our worship and translates it into a powerful testimony, the significance of which we may never know until, in eternity, we see with spiritual eyes the life we have lived.

No Distinctions

The Bible assumes that we will respect all those with whom we worship. The teaching of James is a clear that we are not to give preference in worship based on the visible signs of success and accomplishments. We are called to see but not to judge between observers. Isn't it interesting that the Savior couldn't help but reveal to the disciples that it was the sacrifice rather than the amount given in worship that revealed the widow's great heart?

The circumstances of my walking miracles testify to hearts grown great through faith. Such lives cannot be constrained by their situations. Their faith will not allow their circumstances to define them, but elevates them to a higher plane. If we can only see it, their witness lifts our hearts.

Worship is witness.

❧

I couldn't help but notice them: three obviously homeless men sitting in a back row during worship. Their clothing was worn. Their hats torn and sweat stained. When I walked by them and greeted them, they smelled because they hadn't bathed. Still, when we prayed, their heads bowed low. When we sang hymns that they apparently knew, their voices were strong. And when the greeting was exchanged between worshipers, they crossed the aisle with handshakes that were firm and with smiles that were broad.

After worship, one of our disciples came up to me and said, "Did you see the three men in the back? I think John [our formerly homeless janitor at the time] brought them."

And I cringed. I could imagine him saying, "I don't know why they came here. They belong downtown at the gospel mission, not here in the suburbs."

But this disciple smiled and said, "Isn't it great they're here? Wow . . . I think it says such wonderful things about who we are that John knew we would accept his friends."

I could only agree . . . and confess to a heart that had prejudged a wealthy Christian man and his response to those men who appeared to be poor.

❦

When we worship, we witness to the world. We do not witness to a perfect people. Instead, we witness to frail people who come with the hope of feeling the changing touch of God. In countless communities around the world, Christian worship is a silent but powerful witness to the world that hope still exists—hope for changed human hearts as well as a world changed for good.

I am sad for those outside the Christian Church who perceive that those who worship carry an air of spiritual superiority. I can accept that such arrogance may, indeed, occur, but my experience has been just the opposite. Most of those with whom I have had the privilege of worshiping have come to God acutely aware of their shortcomings. For most of us, worship is all about new beginnings that God promises and gives, beginning with the greatest gift of all: the life and resurrection of Jesus of Nazareth.

When we worship, the Savior takes our faltering voices, our feeble attempts at amendment of life, and makes an oasis of hope in the world. I have often believed that, as long as there are Christians worshiping, this world cannot sink into total despair. For someone, somewhere will watch and take heart. When we worship, we witness to the world of the faithfulness of our God. That's what Dr. Martin Luther King Jr. testified to above.

Worship honors God *before the world*. And the world is changed because of it.

Questions for Reflection

❧ Have you been inspired or touched by seeing someone in worship who was there unexpectedly? What happened?

❧ Describe a time when someone told you, or you have told anyone else, how much it meant that you or they were in worship. Why is it helpful for us to remind one another how good it is to see each other in worship?

❧ How does our worship witness to the world? If you have experienced this, share an example.

V. Worship As Weekly Compass

O Lord, I love the house in which you dwell and the place where your glory abides . . . as for me, I walk in my integrity; redeem me, and be gracious to me. My foot stands on level ground; in the great congregation I will bless the Lord.
    —Psalm 26:8,11-12

Christ, however, was faithful over God's house as a son, and we are his house if we hold firm the confidence and the pride that belong to hope.
    —Hebrews 3:6

Worship liberates the personality by giving a new perspective to life, by integrating life with the multitude of life forms, by bringing in to the

life the virtues of humility, loyalty, devotion, and rightness of attitude,
thus refreshing and reviving our spirits.
　　—Roswell C. Long

It is only when men begin to worship that they begin to grow.
　　—Calvin Coolidge

"I love coming to worship; more than that, I need it. When I get up on Sunday morning and tell my wife I'm going to church, she is happy for me . . . and for herself," he continued. "So often, somewhere between when I wake up and when I begin that forty minute drive to church, I will have had a run in with her. And I'll be convinced that she is the problem. Then I make that drive, and my anger and resentment just get bigger and bigger. But some time, in worship, God will get through and I'll get it: I'll have a mental and spiritual correction. And by the time I get back home," he said with a laugh, "I'll be a different person. Now my wife can't wait for me to come to church every week!"

❧

Worship, for the disciple of Jesus, is not optional. It is essential. The reasons are many, beginning with simple obedience to the Call and Model of Christ. One of the true benefits of weekly worship is that it serves as a "weekly compass" to reorient our lives to that which is good and true. My friend's sharing initially caught me off guard. I had asked the simple question: Why do you come so far to worship with us every week? His response reminded me of the power of God to reshape our souls.

For some of us, like my friend, that often happens in the secret compartment of the human heart reserved for the quiet, gentle touch of the Holy Spirit. He told me he never knows that it will happen, let alone when. But it always does. For others of us, it can come as a hammer breaking the cement of resentments and grudges. Some lives must first have the bulwark of self-righteousness broken first. Then the hand of God can touch and heal and reorient the soul to the good.

I watched as tears flowed down her cheeks. She was sitting in the front row at church, and I couldn't help but notice her strong reaction as I preached. Then, after the service, she slipped up to the altar rail and knelt in prayer, weeping. I guessed she was about twenty-five years of age. Even as the crowds moved around her, still she knelt in tears.

Slowly, I slipped in front of her—allowing enough space so as not to intrude, but close enough so that she could hear me. "Are you all right?" I asked. "Can I help you?"

She looked up and, recognizing me, smiled—though the tears still flowed. "Oh, I feel wonderful." She said. "I haven't been to church in so long, and Jesus touched me so much today. I just wanted time to thank him."

I smiled back. Then she reached out her hand and said, "But Pastor Mike, could you pray that God will give me the strength to live my faith? I have so many friends who don't believe, and it's hard to keep believing, let alone share my faith. Pray that I can come back to worship soon and that I'll be bold in sharing my faith—will you?"

So kneeling with her, we prayed.

❧

A weekly compass can be as startling as that touch of God in that young woman's heart. Or it can be as gentle as a reminder that we worship a God whose very character is loyalty, devotion, humility, and rightness of judgment. God calls us to a life of purpose. Our life's meaning can only be discovered as we are oriented and then reoriented to these essential and good qualities.

Life purpose is not haphazard, nor is it always easy to discover. We are called to weekly worship so that we might grow in our awareness and practice of these discipleship virtues.

To be human is to lose our way in the noise and busy-ness of our lives. And the daily-ness of life can pull us away from what we really believe, drag us away from how we long to behave, or seduce us into following after all the lesser goods that clamor for our allegiance. Weekly worship is a heaven-sent compass to reorient our lives and point us to spiritual "true north."

When I practice worship as a spiritual compass, I strive to live a five-step process:

The first step is to take a moment, as I enter worship, to reflect on the occasions of anger and hurt from the past week. I try to name them honestly before God.

The second step is for God to show me "my stuff." I pray that the Holy Spirit will show me what I did that I need to own and learn from. I also ask for the spiritual wisdom to discern what is "their stuff"; that is, what I cannot and should not take on to myself because it belongs to someone else, or the circumstances of that time. (My experience is that Christians often, after initially blaming another, will take far too much responsibility for those things that are beyond our control and belong to others.)

The third step is to pray for the persons involved. I lift them up to God asking God to heal and bless them, even as I ask God to heal and bless me by taking the anger and hurt and preventing them from becoming grudges.

The fourth step is to ask God to tell me what would be a healthy response to those events. Sometimes, the best response is none at all! There are times when, in an attempt to heal a relationship or put a conflict behind us, we act and make it more of a burden to the other than is necessary or helpful. There are other times when, to re-enter that relationship for any reason, is to be vulnerable to more attacks or abuse. But there are other times when God has made it clear through the function of my own con-science, that I must make amends.

The last step is to develop a strategy for making amends when that seems necessary. I want to initiate the conversation by owning my own failings. I want to have the conversation some-where and sometime when the other person and I can deal with it together. Then, as the last step, I commit myself to acting on that strategy.

☙❧

This is a form of confession, in its best sense. Sometimes, I have sinned against myself. I have behaved in ways that have not been healthy to my body or mind or spirit. Then I strive to right my life through the reorienting of my moral compass.

God commands worship. The disciple fully understands that our God, whose loyalty to us has proven timeless, will never expect of us anything that is not good and to our spiritual bene-fit. Weekly worship is a rich deposit of gifts. God invites us to mine that spiritual deposit. This honors God and grows abundant, purpose-filled life within us as well.

Questions for Reflection

❧ What do you think of the idea that "worship is not optional"?

❧ How is weekly worship like a compass? What other words or metaphors would you use to describe worship?

❧ How do you "approach" worship? Does worship meet your expectations? Why or why not?

CHAPTER 3

HEARING GOD'S VOICE

THE MARK OF DISCIPLESHIP:
DAILY BIBLE READING

I. More Than Mere Words

Happy are those who do not follow the advice of the wicked . . . their delight is in the law of the Lord, and on his law they meditate day and night. They are like trees planted by streams of water, which yield their fruit in its season, and their leaves do not wither.
    —Psalm 1:1-3

One does not live by bread alone, but by every word that comes from the mouth of God.
    —Matthew 4:4

Other books were given for our information; the Bible was given for our transformation.
    —The Defender

The third practice of the disciple is Daily Bible Reading. This Mark of Discipleship reminds us that true spiritual growth comes as we are planted in the rich soil of God's Word. As our Savior said, we live not only through physical provision, but through the nourishment of the soul. Reading the Bible daily speaks to the eternal longings within each human heart. More than that, the words come to life within us as we receive the Word of God, and we come to life as the words and the voice of God echo within us.

❧❧

"I wish I had your Bible," she said, after the Bible study I had led that Monday night.

"What do you mean?" I asked. "You and I have the very same translation."

"Well, maybe we do," she continued, "but my Bible doesn't tell me all the things that yours tells you. You get so much more out of it than I ever see. So I wish I had your Bible instead of mine."

"Well," I said, "I've had some great Bible teachers in my life. So you get the benefit of their wisdom in what I see and share."

❧❧

The Bible speaks when disciples approach it with a listening heart and an inquiring mind. One of the great myths of our society is the idea that faith is the absence of thinking or that questioning is the same as unbelief. Interesting. As I read of the life of Jesus, I never see him angrily dismissing any real question. Instead, the Savior honors even the most difficult questions when they are authentic. The inauthentic questions that are asked of him in order to trap him are dismissed with disdain.

When God invites us to read and study the Word, God doesn't require us to understand everything. Nor does God invite us to the Scriptures to solve all of our problems. God invites us into a relationship through the words of the Bible, and that relationship is primarily with God's Son, Jesus, whom we call the Living Word.

The Holy Spirit uses the words of the Bible to present to us the heart and character of God. Christians understand that Jesus has come to embody God's heart and character. So when God speaks in and through the Bible, God directs our attention to Christ. God never speaks a word to us through the Bible that contradicts or supplants what Jesus did or taught.

How do we discover the abundant life promised by Jesus? We must grow deep in our understanding of the Scriptures. The depth of our understanding opens more of the words of the Bible to us. My Bible wasn't saying anything that my friend's Bible didn't say. The only difference was my familiarity with the words and my searching through the words for God's voice to me. This was a process that my friend had barely become familiar with, let alone used.

How can a disciple truly hear the voice of God in the words of the Bible? How can we be certain that our understanding isn't just our own limited thinking? The Christian Church has historically offered a three-step process for such listening and discerning:

First, in a quiet place where you will not be interrupted, begin to pray that God would speak to you in the words you are going to read in the Bible. Tell God that your desire is not information, but the transformation of your soul. Invite the Holy Spirit to open God's heart and character to you in the words of Scripture.

Second, read the passage, stopping when it speaks to you or when you have reached the end of that section. Then ask these few questions. What does this passage tell me about God or life? How does what I hear fit with what I know about Jesus—his life and teaching, death and resurrection? What life lesson is here for me?

The third step is to pray that God will plant deeply within you the words that make for life. These are those words and lessons that you can then "wear" for a season. By "wearing the words" I mean that we can put the Bible on like a robe over our hearts and minds. We want to conform our attitudes and behaviors to what we have received. So we ask God for the gift of the Holy Spirit to empower us to do this.

If a passage remains "speechless" for you, then simply continue your reading until the Bible speaks to you or you reach the end of another section. If a passage is more confusing than helpful, move on in the Scriptures. You can always ask God for help in receiving a clear word through the Bible. If you are confused, you can, as I often do, simply give that passage to God, trusting that God will make known in time what you might need to hear from the text.

This form of Bible reading is not for information. By that I mean that knowledge about the Bible has little or nothing to do with the disciple's growth in spiritual understanding of the Bible. It can be helpful to establish context and provide insight from ancient cultures and languages, but such background reading cannot provide the experience of hearing God's voice through the words of the Bible. If such information were essential for our spiritual growth, then translating the Bible into the common vernacular, making it accessible to everyone, would not be a good idea. The Christian Church has universally affirmed that God can speak to anyone in and through the Bible—so it ought to be available to all who desire to read it.

Questions for Reflection

❧ How is the Bible "spiritual nourishment" for you?

❧ How does comparing individual passages to the life and teaching of Jesus help us? How can it be a help in discerning God's voice from our own inner voice?

❧ Explain in your own words the distinction between biblical knowledge and biblical understanding? How is such a distinction helpful for your reading?

❧ Describe a time when you read a passage and truly heard the voice of God in and through it? What happened? Have you ever told anyone else about it?

II. The Voice of God in the Words of People

All scripture is inspired by God and is useful for teaching, for reproof, for correction, and for training in righteousness.
   —2 Timothy 3:16

No prophecy of scripture is a matter of one's own interpretation, because no prophecy ever came by human will, but men and women moved by the Holy Spirit spoke from God.
   —2 Peter 1:20-21

Apply yourself to the whole text, and apply the whole text to yourself.
   —J. A. Bengel

The Bible is criticized most by those who read it least.
   —Anonymous

"You know, Pastor Mike," he said, "you've convinced me that I should read the Bible regularly. But I don't know how or where to begin. I have three Bibles at home, and two of them are still in their boxes!" he said with a smile. "So is there a better translation? Where do I start? And don't tell me to start at the beginning and read it all the way through. I don't get all that creation stuff."

One of the remarkable aspects of a discipleship ministry is that we meet those who have been called to faith with little or no religious background, let alone Christian education. Once, those of us who are in Christian ministry could expect a minimal level Bible literacy, now we need to start at a new "point A." Even for those who have had a significant amount of Christian education, the awakening to discipleship opens a new spiritual world. Their perceptions of God's word are often distorted by intellectual assumptions that get in the way of hearing the voice of God in the words of men and women.

So where do we start?

First, we are so blessed to have many good translations available to us today. Any of the newer translations of the Bible will do. Most modern translations are based on the original Hebrew and Greek languages, and understanding subtle differences in translations is based on serious study of these languages. The introduction in the front of a particular Bible will help you understand who the translators were and some factors that make the translation unique. Still, you do not have to be a Greek or Hebrew scholar to study the Bible. Translations are created with great care, and you can trust them. However, a Bible that goes a step beyond a translation is known as a *paraphrase*. In such a version, the author may add his or her own interpretation of what the Bible text really says. You should be aware that when you read a paraphrase, you will be getting more than a straight translation of the original languages. I always recommend beginning with a translation rather than a paraphrase, but choose one in which the language can easily be understood and appreciated.

Next, I suggest that a person ask what kind of life lessons might be particularly interesting or helpful. The *Life Application Bible* and *The Leadership Bible* both have notes that make the application of a particular passage for the reader. These applications are never the only ones that can be made, nor are they the best. But they can help a reader learn the process of listening to the Bible for life insights that make a real difference.

I also encourage those who are beginning to read the Bible to know the difference between devotional and scholastic reading of the Bible. These forms differ by intent. The scholastic reading is focused on knowledge about the writer, the historical context, and the theological framework or contribution of the book. A devotional reading will focus on hearing the text for the spiritual growth of the individual. These can be complimentary to one another, but they are not the same. In either case, pay little or no attention to the verse or chapter numbering system. These were added late to the text and serve only one purpose—to help us locate a particular book and passage with ease. And if a person is interested in a scholastic reading, I recommend one of a number of study Bibles, such as *The Oxford Annotated Bible*, *NIV Study Bible*, *HarperCollins Study Bible*, or *Contemporary English Version Learning Bible*, which has a great number of articles, charts, maps, and notes designed to help novice Bible readers.

I also recommend beginning with one of the Gospels, preferably Luke or Mark. These present a clear portrait of the Savior and are readily accessible to the contemporary reader. Reading from the book of Psalms can be a wonderful foray into the heart of Old Testament spirituality. The New Testament letters of Paul and James can extend the spiritual awareness of the reader. Readings in the Old Testament sometimes take a bit more background to understand, as the history of God's interaction with the chosen people of Israel is presented in many different kinds of literature from stories to history to prophetic writings, and wisdom. This is where a good study Bible can provide helpful background for understanding the key themes of the Old Testament.

God's Word Is Inspired

So how can we be attentive to the voice of God in the words of human beings?

First, recognize what inspiration means. It does not mean that God used human beings like a "dicta-phone." By that I mean that God's respect and love for all human beings includes the writers of the books! God uses the personalities and life experiences of the writers through the Bible's texts. Paul will not sound like Peter. Nor will Mark's Gospel read like John's Gospel. God uses the unique witness of each person—voice and style—just as God will use each of us to witness in our own words and personality.

Second, we recognize that there is a progression in the Word. The language of Genesis is not the language of Matthew. The literature of Proverbs will not correspond to that of Revelation. This may seem obvious, but it is helpful as we read. This also means that, although we believe that God is unchanging, our awareness of God and the world is not. The core of Scripture, for Christians, is Jesus. He holds our changing perceptions of God together. Whatever we read or hear, we know that its spiritual truth will be born out in comparison to Jesus and to what he taught and did, as well as to the doctrines and traditions of the historic Christian Church—and in that order.

In this way the judgment of God in the Old Testament is reinterpreted by the life and teaching of Jesus in the New Testament. God could always judge the world by some kind of divine intervention, but according to the New Testament, God chose to act by means of his son Jesus, who came to forgive and to provide a way for all to become children of God. Still, the salvation offered in Jesus for human beings extends to the world. God cares about all creation and expects his people to care for creation and all people. In this way, God's concern for justice remains. God has acted to forgive, but this does not eliminate God's judgment.

Third, read each passage as part of God's whole story. God's story is about reaching out to us and about God's deep desire to have a relationship with us and to empower us to live an abundant life—a life with significance and purpose. So we read devotionally to know about God, the human condition, and the world so that we can discover this wonderful will of our God for our lives. When this happens, we will have heard the voice of God through the power of the Holy Spirit. When it doesn't seem to happen, keep reading—it will come.

So approach your reading with the expectation that God has something wonderful to say to you. Read and ponder. Reflect on what this or that passage might say to how you are living and how you are relating to Jesus, to others, and to yourself. For example, the Commandments of God are understood to be gifts for a healthy focus for living. They provide guidelines for how we can live in healthier relationship to God and to one another. When we fail, we are drawn into repentance and forgiveness—the Christian process of new beginnings.

So reading the Bible is always a celebration of new beginnings! This is the place where we can personally meet God and grow in confident trust in the presence and will of our heavenly Father. In this way, the Bible speaks to the eternal longings given to each human soul.

Questions for Reflection

❧ How did you start reading the Bible?

❧ How have you heard the voice of God in the words of people?

❧ How is God's concern for justice reveled in the Old and New Testaments? How are these ideas complementary?

❧ How can the Commandments of God be seen as helpful?

III. Praying the Scriptures

This is the covenant that I will make with the house of Israel after those days, says the Lord: I will put my law within them, and I will write it on their hearts.
　—Jeremiah 31:33

Go and learn what this means, "I desire mercy, not sacrifice. For I have come to call not the righteous but sinners."
　—Matthew 9:13

What is home without a Bible?
'Tis a home where daily bread
For the body is provided,
But the soul is never fed.
　—C. D. Meigs

The Bible is a window in this prison world,
Through which we may look into eternity.
　—Timothy Dwight

No matter how late he had returned to his home, my maternal grandfather would end the day by reading the Bible in his rocking chair next to a lit floor lamp. I can still see him sitting there. He would read and talk to himself at the same time. When I was young I assumed that it was because, as an Iowa farmer, he had little formal education and had to say the words out loud. Later I would learn that he had successfully attended college!

What my grandfather would do was both argue with and pray through the Scriptures. His was an active faith. He met God in the Bible and held conversation with Jesus as he read. He embraced the Word and tried to discern it. Only later, at seminary, did

I learn a marvelous way of reading the Bible: Praying the Scriptures, much like my grandfather did.

What is praying the Scriptures and how do we practice it? First, I believe it fulfills the promise of God through the prophet Jeremiah quoted above. As we pray through a passage, the Bible's message is written on our hearts. We draw close to God through this practice and begin to "own" the passage itself.

Second, I believe that as we pray the Scriptures we ask the Holy Spirit to tutor us in the meaning of the Word. It is an act of obedience to the teaching of the Savior. Praying the Bible is like digesting a spiritual meal. It is no longer outside of us. Like food nourishes our bodies, Scripture reading and study nourishes our souls.

The process for praying the Scriptures is simple. We take a passage and, with each part, turn it into prayer. For example, let us take that remarkable passage called the Beatitudes found in the Sermon on the Mount. We read:

Blessed are the poor in spirit, for theirs is the kingdom
    of heaven.

Blessed are those who mourn, for they will be comforted.

Blessed are the meek, for they will inherit the earth.

Blessed are those who hunger and thirst for righteousness,
    for they will be filled.

Blessed are the merciful, for they will receive mercy.

Blessed are the pure in heart, for they will see God.

Blessed are the peacemakers, for they will be called the
    children of God.

Blessed are those who are persecuted for righteousness'
    sake, for theirs is the kingdom of heaven.

(Matthew 5:3-10)

After reading the passage, take a moment to simply reflect upon it. Let the words echo in your mind. Then begin praying through each Beatitude in words like this:

Lord Jesus, I am so thankful that you have given to us these great teachings. I pray that your Holy Spirit will help me to understand and receive your teaching. I pray that I will grow to understand my own poverty in spirit so that I can turn to you and thereby inherit the kingdom. I pray for those who are poor in spirit and do not know you. Help me as a disciple to be open to loving them and sharing your love with them in a way that will be a truthful witness to you. I pray for those whose poverty of spirit is lost to them. They may think that they have it all, but are lacking in spiritual openness. Open them to your truth, and empower your church throughout the world to be humble in its words and deeds, first aware that without you and your grace we are poor indeed. Amen

꙳

This form of praying can be used in almost any passage. There are four steps in this process:

꙳ Thank God for the truth and power of the words we have read.

꙳ Ask God through the power of the Holy Spirit to open us to them so that we not only read but also can live them.

꙳ Pray for others within the context of our understanding of the text.

꙳ Recall the universal community of faith through which we have received the Bible and its witness.

Reading the Bible on a daily or regular basis connects us to the greatest story of all time—God's seeking humankind in love and truth. Second, such reading connects us to the community of faith that has come to us throughout the centuries. And lastly, by praying the Scriptures we can connect us to the world—to humanity or all created things.

Questions for Reflection

❧ Have you ever argued or talked to God when you read the Bible?

❧ What benefits would praying the Scriptures provide for you or others?

❧ How might praying the Scriptures be a part of weekly worship?

❧ How does praying the Scriptures remind us that the Bible is for our growth within community?

IV. Meeting Jesus in the Bible: *Lectio Divina*

But as for (the seed) in the good soil, these are the ones who, when they hear the word, hold it fast in an honest and good heart, and bear fruit with patient endurance.

—Luke 8:15

O that my people would listen to me, that Israel would walk in my ways!
—Psalm 81:13

It matters not how oft you kneel
In attitude of prayer so true,
Unless inside, where no man sees,
Your very soul is kneeling too.
—Mary L. O'Hara

Whatever happens, abide steadfast in a determination to cling simply to God.
—Francis de Sales

One of the great ways to meet the Savior through the reading of the Bible is called *Lectio Divina*. This gift is best discovered and used in community, although it can be done by one's self.

The process is simple. A passage of Scripture is chosen and read aloud, usually three times with a period of silence after each reading. Those who hear it are asked to listen for the voice of Jesus. How? By focusing in on that word or phrase that strikes an inner chord and imagine that it is Jesus who is speaking to you. Then follow your thoughts as they progress around and from those words. Meditate on the words. Let your heart seek the divine word (hence the name *Lectio Divina*) from Jesus to you. This form of meditation usually takes time—at least twenty minutes for the readings, silence and prayerful reflection. It is best to have someone read the words and allow you to hear them, not read them yourself. This auditory style of Bible reading not only places us within Christian community but it encourages us to hear that inner voice of God.

A word of caution must be added here. How do we differentiate our own thinking from the voice of God? There are three tests I suggest for simplicity's sake:

First, how does what you hear lift your soul up to the majesty and wonder of God in the crucified and risen Christ? If it doesn't, it is most likely your own thinking.

Second, how does what you hear move you to thoughts, attitudes, and actions that fit the person and work of Jesus? Jesus never tore down without seeking to build up. Jesus never spoke or acted in a manner that didn't invite those around him to a closer walk with God and to an abundant life. If your prayerful reflection leads you to destructive attitudes or actions against yourself or another, then they are not inspired by the Holy Spirit speaking in the voice of Jesus within you.

I remember with a deep sadness reading the tragic story of a young man in Washington State. He was in deep spiritual and mental turmoil and opened the Bible for guidance. Unfortunately, his eyes fell upon the teaching of Jesus that it is better to cut off one's hand or pluck out one's eyeball and enter heaven maimed than to go to hell in one piece. So he attempted both actions! Yet Jesus never asked anyone to do such a thing. This teaching is a use of exaggeration as a teaching tool, and is not to be taken literally, as that young man did. When what we read or hear does not match up to how Jesus lived or expected others to live, then it is not of God.

Lastly, how does what you hear move you to reconciliation? The voice of God calls us to be reconciled to our sisters and brothers. We are even told to love and pray for our enemies. If your experience of *Lectio Divina* does not move you to forgiving others and striving to seek healing in your relationships, then you have not heard the voice of God. The fruits of Christ's voice are numbered by Saint Paul as the fruits of the Spirit—love, joy, peace, patience, kindness, generosity, faithfulness, gentleness, and self-control (Galatians 5:22-23).

My prayer is that, as you try this way of reading God's word, you will experience the words of the Bible washing over and refreshing you like the waters of Holy Baptism. I pray that you will hear the voice of the Good Shepherd calling you by name and touching you with his eternal love for you and all creation.

Questions for Reflection

❧ Have you ever listened to the Bible being read and felt like God was speaking just to you? What happened? What did you do with it?

❧ Describe a time when you were reading the Bible and a phrase or word leapt out at you and captured your attention. What was that experience like?

❧ Consider gathering with a group of Jesus' disciples to share the experience of reading Scripture aloud so that the others could listen. Talk about what happens in this reading and then pray with those who have gathered.

V. Living in the Word of God

Hear, O Israel: the Lord is our God, the Lord alone. You shall love your God with all your heart, and with all your soul and with all your might. Keep these words that I am commanding you today in your heart. Recite them to your children and talk about them when you are at home and when you are away, when you lie down and when you rise. Bind them as a sign on your hand, fix them as an emblem on your forehead, and write them on the doorposts of your house and on your gates.
    —Deuteronomy 6:4-9

Your word is a lamp to my feet and a light to my path.
    —Psalm 119:105

Jesus answered him, "Those who love me will keep my word, and my Father will love them, and we will come to them and make our home with them."
    —John 14:23

Many people are bothered by those passages in Scripture, which they cannot understand; but as for me, I always noticed that the passages that trouble me most are those which I do understand.
    —Mark Twain

The Bible is a great and powerful tree. Each word is a mighty branch. Each of these branches I will have shaken. And the shaking of them has never disappointed me.
    —Martin Luther

"I can't believe it! You want me to forgive her?" he said. His anger and hurt were palpable. He had just shared with me how his wife had betrayed him. He had discovered that she had been having an affair at work for many months. And when he finally told her she had to choose, she walked out, leaving him with two small children.

As I listened and felt his pain, he told me that he needed to move on—for his children's sake and for his own sake. But he couldn't. The pain and anger were touched off every time he saw her, talked with her on the phone and waved good-bye to his children when she came to pick them up for her time with them.

"You've got to forgive her," I said. But he lost it. His eyes filled with tears, his face grew red, and he just exploded.

I waited for him to calm down and then continued. "You know, Jesus commands us to forgive. And I don't think it has much to do with the one we forgive. It can, but we have no control over that. I believe that Jesus commands us to forgive because it is the only way we can get free of what has happened to us."

"So I'm supposed to pretend it never happened?" he asked. "I can't do that."

"Jesus Christ never asks us to set aside our feelings . . . at least not initially. You don't forgive people who haven't sinned against you. Only God can really forgive and forget."

"So how does this forgiveness work?" he asked.

"Well, forgiveness is, biblically speaking, a three-step process. First you decide to trust the Savior and forgive her. Then you begin to live *as if* the forgiveness has happened. That empowers you to get some emotional distance, and you can begin to learn from what has happened. As that occurs, the third aspect of forgiveness evolves—your feelings catch up with your faith."

"So I don't have to forget what happened or pretend about it? I can forgive even when I don't feel like it?" he asked.

"Well, you know the Bible and the teaching of Jesus. Do you really believe that Jesus would ask you to do something that is both impossible for you to do and hurtful to you?"

"No, I don't," he whispered.

"So let the Bible support you and forgive your former wife. That's when you'll begin to get free from the past that is imprisoning you."

🕊🕊

I love Mark Twain's quote on page 72. The truth of the matter is that we begin to live in the Word of God when we can see how it calls us to freedom and peace, when we are least interested in them or able to see them as possibilities. As we read the Bible daily, we begin to discover how the Scriptures speak into our real life issues and circumstances.

This Christian man had given his past enormous power over him. By extension, the one who he had come to distrust the most, his former wife, was given power over his feelings that she didn't even want. The Bible became a living truth when he could face the command of Jesus to forgive precisely in his situation. It was the last thing he wanted to do but the first thing he needed to do.

The people who bind the Word of God to their lives (which is how I understand the Deuteronomy to be interpreted) look to it in every circumstance. They bind it on their heart by trusting that God doesn't ask of us what we cannot do. They bind it on their arm by then exercising obedience to live from the eternal strength of God's word, as they best understand it. And they write it over their homes and gates by seeking in the Bible those things that make for healthy relationships with family and friends.

When was the last time that the Bible spoke to you in a situation, and you didn't want to hear it? Did you follow it or—as we all have done—did you turn away from it seeking another, easier, less painful way of responding to your circumstances? If you did the latter, as I have done so many times, then did it really lead to freedom and a new beginning? Most of the time it does not.

Reading the Bible daily equips us to live in the Word of God. This connects us to God's loving design or purpose for our lives. And if we truly believe that God desires nothing less than that we have life and have it in abundance, then the Bible will only guide us to make the decisions that lead to such a life over time.

My friend chose to forgive his wife and, over time, he could even be civil to her. More than that, over time he could see how she was a loving and caring mother. That began to free him up to date others and, in a few years after that initial conversation, God blessed him with a wonderful life partner.

Living out God's word and seeking the will of God in the Scriptures is a clear Mark of Discipleship. Without a consistent connection with the Bible, we can lose our way and miss out on the grace and abundance God offers.

Questions for Reflection

❧ Which passages of the Bible trouble you the most—the ones you don't understand or the ones you do? Why?

❧ What is your reaction to the threefold process of forgiveness described above? Is it something that you could actually do?

❧ Which idea or ideas in this chapter were most beneficial to you? Why?

❧ In what circumstances have you found the Bible's teaching to be most helpful?

CHAPTER 4

THE CALL TO
CHRISTLIKE LIVING

THE MARK OF DISCIPLESHIP: SERVING IN AND BEYOND THE CONGREGATION

I. Created to Serve

You shall be for me a priestly kingdom and a holy nation.
　　—Exodus 19:6

The Spirit of the Lord is upon me, to bring good news to the poor.
　　—Luke 4:18

God loves the world through you and me.
　　—Mother Teresa

All the beautiful sentiments in the world weigh less than a single lovely action.
　　—James Russell Lowell

"Happy Thanksgiving!" my wife and I said, as the people entered the dining room. It was Thanksgiving Day, and we had come to the Salvation Army to serve meals to the homeless of Minneapolis. And they came. Adults of all generations and children came for hot turkey and dressing, mashed potatoes and gravy, yams, and fresh pumpkin pie with whipped cream.

As we greeted them, I noticed that most of them would look down at the floor as we shook hands, as if ashamed of having to be at the Salvation Army for Thanksgiving. I began to bend down and make eye contact whenever I greeted an adult. And that's when things began to change. People smiled. They began to talk to one another, and there was even laughter in that dining room. I have never forgotten how many of them sought us out to say thank you after they had eaten.

❦

The last three Marks of Discipleship signal a shift in the disciple's practices. These call us outward to the world. The fourth Mark of Discipleship is Serving in and beyond the Congregation. That's what my wife and I were doing at the Salvation Army on that Thanksgiving Day. We had come to serve anonymously; only the head cook, my cousin, knew who we were.

Though they lived on the edge, those whom we served were not anonymous. How they had made it through long cold nights on the street was beyond me. As they came to receive a hot meal, both my wife and I knew that these were not anonymous faces to God. Jesus knew them and, according to Scripture, came to us in each one. And perhaps, an angel or two passed through those doors.

That's why I couldn't just let them pass, eyes downcast in shame. How can there be shame in poverty? Simple. In our country, we assume that poverty is the mark of personal failure, the consequence of a character flaw. In some cases that may be true. But God does not see only the failure or flaw. We believe that God sees each person as an eternal investment in this world. And God never gives up on any of us.

The call to serve is the command of the Savior to allow God's love to flow through us into our love-starved world. Disciples serve because when we grow deep in relationship to the Savior, he brings with him other people. Jesus never comes to us without bringing others with him. And as we have been loved, so we are called to love.

This is our purpose as the people of God. We are called to be a priestly people, priests who serve others on behalf of God. Their serving is essential to their calling and role. Serving others in Jesus' name is just as essential to our identity as Christian disciples.

This is also one of the points at which our joy is activated. Again and again, I have heard those who serve in a significant way tell me what I have personally experienced: when we serve we receive so much more than we give. On that Thanksgiving Day, my wife and I left with a deep gratitude for the honor of serving. The thankful responses of those whom we had greeted and served were echoing in our hearts. That was a Thanksgiving that we have never forgotten—not so much because of what we had given but by what we had received.

Christians believe that all human beings have been created in the image of God. God is the original server. Creation itself is the first act of God's serving. Physicists call it the "sympathetic principle." This universe has been created in sympathy to our lives. All that has been created has been structured in such a way that life as we know it can exist. God created time and space; the sun, moon, and stars; water, air, and earth so that life could thrive. Creation is God's serving heart in action.

Jesus came to serve, and not to be served. The essence of God is love in serving action. We cannot know God apart from God's serving love for us. If human beings are created in the image of God, incomplete as that image is, then serving is at the heart of who we are. There is no purpose to your life or mine without acts of serving. In those actions, we discover the best of ourselves. That is why when we serve we receive so much more than we give. In our serving, we connect to that heaven-sent impulse that is a part of God's image within us. So our soul's deepest longings are expressed when we serve.

One of my personal heroes is Mother Teresa. Her life was spent in serving. She wandered the streets of Calcutta by herself in the early days of her ministry. Soon her personal expression of God's love for the "poorest of the poor" was so compelling that others from around the world would join her. For her, it was never enough simply to bring respite to the dying or food to the starving individual. There was also an intense desire to communicate the personal value of that individual before God. In other words, she gave dignity to those whose lives had none.

I would like to think that my personal knowledge and reverence for her work was expressed as I began to systematically bend down to catch the eyes of those who entered the Salvation Army that Thanksgiving Day. By making an effort to look them in the eyes while I greeted them warmly, I was attempting to demonstrate their value, their dignity. How often do we walk past such persons as if they don't exist? If that is a person's primary experience in society, then she or he will soon believe that, in the deepest sense of the word, they do not exist. God calls the disciple to intervene with acts of compassion and mercy in a manner that reasserts every individual's eternal value in Jesus Christ.

Questions for Reflection

❧ Describe a time when you served others and walked away having the sense that you had received so much more than you had given?

🔊 Do you agree or disagree that part of the image of God within each person is the need to serve?

🔊 What do you think of God's creation as God's first act of service?

🔊 How important is serving in a way that asserts the dignity of those served? Why?

II. Serving God's People

Now there are varieties of gifts, but the same Spirit; and there are varieties of services, but the same Lord; and there are varieties of activities, but it is the same God who activates all of them in everyone.
    —1 Corinthians 12:4-6

Whoever wishes to become great among you must be your servant, and whoever wishes to be first among you must be slave of all. For the Son of Man came not to be served but to serve, and to give his life as a ransom for many.
    —Mark 10:43-45

God sends no churches from the skies,
Out of our hearts they must arise.
    —Anonymous

The church exists to train its members through the practice of the presence of God to be servants of others, to the end that Christlikeness may become common property.
    —William Adams Brown

"Pastor Mike, I really want to be involved here at Prince of Peace, but I don't want to teach Sunday school!" she said.

"Well, what we really want to do is match you to your gifts and passions. What do you love to do?" I replied.

"You know, no one in all the churches I have attended ever asked that question. Let me think," she said and then became silent. "I guess I'd love to do research or read books or something like that, but I bet you don't have any ways for me to serve here doing that!"

"As a matter of fact we do. Or more precisely, I do. I need research assistants and readers to find and digest significant articles and presentations on topics of interest. Would you be willing to do that? Because, if you would, I have some things you could do for me that would help my preaching and teaching, staff development, and vision process right away!"

"You've got to be kidding," she said. "I always thought that serving in the congregation meant that I had to do something like teach Sunday school! You mean that I can serve this church by doing things that I really like to do?"

"Well, yes, that's exactly what I would hope we could all discover. I know there will be times when we will need to step out of our comfort zone to meet a real need, but I also believe that God has already prepared us for service in the church, and it begins with understanding what we love to do and the spiritual gifts we have been given."

"I don't know anything about spiritual gifts," she said softly.

"Let me invite you to our LifeKeys class. It's great! You'll learn wonderful things about yourself that you never knew before, and things you knew but didn't understand will become clearer for you."

❧

In the 1 Corinthians text on page 80, the apostle Paul assumes a number of very important things. The first is that we are all gifted. God has gifted us with talents (what I like to call gifts of creation because we are born with them ready to be discovered and developed) and spiritual gifts (gifts that only the Holy Spirit can give, such as discernment). To those we need to add those things that "stoke our fires." These are our passions and strong interests. Paul tells us that the church, the body of Christ, ought to be one of the places where these significant parts of ourselves are developed and used. In fact, he is so passionate about it that he spends a great deal of time telling us that any service or act or sharing we give to the congregation is, in fact, a special provision of Almighty God.

Interesting. When was the last time any of us in the church actually thought that our gifts, talents, and passions could be set loose for ministry within the congregation? Unfortunately, I have had countless conversations like the one I had with that woman in my office. Most Christians believe that serving in the congregation is half duty and half perseverance! There's no joy in that!

As I have said elsewhere, Jesus Christ calls us to an abundant life. Service within the church that is dispassionate and plodding simply doesn't fit. In fact, if that has been your experience in the congregation, I urge you to say no and look for a much more significant area of serving.

Don't just walk away. We have grown to express the church's need for each of our gifts in entirely institutional needs. How tragic! The old time and talent forms were worse than useless. More often than not they made the promise that those who filled them out would be contacted, while the actual reality was that they were culled for the specific needs of the programming and otherwise discarded.

The Bible assumes that you and I will give significant time and effort for the strengthening and spiritual vitality of the congregation. This is non-negotiable. But, as in all the commands of the Bible, this one is met with a promise. The promise is that your gifts and passions will make a significant contribution—and you'll see it!

I remember only two or three Sunday school teachers in my life. The earliest is a Sunday school teacher whose face I can still see, but whose name I have long since forgotten. I went to her class because it was held at a church close to my house. I remember few things about that church—I was only four or five at the time—but I remember her.

You see, when I was five years old I was admitted to the hospital with appendicitis. And this teacher visited me in the hospital, even though it was in a town one-half hour away. I'll never forget it; she gave me a little plaque of the Psalm 23. In my mind's eye I can still see that plaque: brown scroll with white lettering. But it wasn't the plaque that meant so much. It was that a woman I barely knew would take the time to bring Sunday school to me in a hospital far away. I'm sure that her caring and passion for her children wasn't limited to me, but it made a lasting impression on me.

Her passion for sharing Jesus with children is obvious, don't you think? And perhaps in my own passion for sharing Jesus with others, I have reflected a small part of her heart. I hope so.

So taking time to give of yourself in the local church is an incredible opportunity to influence the lives of others. Some of us will share our faith and serve through teaching or leading a youth group. For others of us, it may be ushering on Sunday or Saturday night, mowing the church lawn, or preparing the bread, wine, and grape juice for Holy Communion.

God connects us with the kingdom of heaven when we serve in the church. Our time and effort do not go unnoticed by the Savior who is Lord of the church. He who sees even the smallest of our contributions smiles and blesses us for them.

The power of the local congregation is not to be measured simply by the visible gathering of its people. It is measured also by the way its people expand and extend the kingdom of God into a world of skepticism, loneliness, and need. The service we give in the congregation, whether highly visible or relatively hidden, spreads the truth of God through the best witness possible: the lives of those who we touch by the power of God's Holy Spirit.

If you are not serving in your church you are missing part of the eternal purpose God intends for you. Your service will be measured not in terms of hours in preparation or serving, but in the invisible touch you have on the lives of others.

Questions for Reflection

❧ Has serving the congregation meant joy and the sharing of your gifts and passions? Or has it been, mostly, drudgery? Why?

❧ What do you see as your strongest gifts and interests? How can these be used in your congregation to serve others?

❧ What would happen if your church were organized for serving based on people's true interests and gifts rather than simply on what the program needs of the congregation happened to be? What would it look like?

❧ Consider the lives you and others can touch through your congregational serving? Think of one person who has touched your life through their serving in congregational ministry. What ministries of service are yet to be discovered?

III. Meeting Real Needs within the Church

I give you a new commandment, that you love one another. Just as I have loved you, you also should love one another. By this everyone will know that you are my disciples, if you have love for one another.
   —John 13:34-35

If any think they are religious, and do not bridle their tongues but deceive their hearts, their religion is worthless.
   —James 1:26

He cannot have God for his Father who refuses to have the Church for his mother.
   —St. Augustine

A church is a hospital for sinners, not a museum for saints.
   —Abigail Van Buren

"You know, I can't serve in the church," he said.

"Why is that?" I asked.

"Well, the last time I served in the church, I got involved in a congregational fight. It was ugly. I never thought Christians could behave that way—and toward one another!"

"I am sorry for your experience, but the church isn't perfect, is it?" I asked.

"No," he replied with a grin, "but the last time I got really involved it was a little too imperfect!"

"But that doesn't change the fact that we have a real need, and your efforts can help us a lot. We need someone with your abilities to organize if we are going to gather the food and clothing necessary for this family whose house has burned down. Will you help us? It is very important work and, once it is over, you can tell me if it was worth it or not."

"Well, for the sake of that family I'll give it a try. But I hope it is a much better experience than my last one was!" And our conversation ended.

🐾

One of the incredible gifts of working within the church is that real needs are present. We live in a world where need and desire are often confused. But my experience in the church is that pastors and lay leaders alike try very hard to separate out the bogus from the authentic when it comes to real need.

Most of the time, when a real need is present, disciples of Jesus demonstrate a remarkable ability to set aside their grievances and differences and pull together to meet the need. In fact, I don't believe there is a more human and yet more effective group of people or institution in meeting the real needs of others than the Christian church!

Please take note of the two parts of the equation I stated above. Both *more human* and *more effective*. "Christians," as a bumper sticker I saw once declared, "aren't perfect . . . just forgiven." And that is very true. I have known people in the church who griped about not having more volunteers and then, when others were recruited for them, they closed them out of service. Thank goodness that seldom happens. In fact, most of us are thankful for the addition of another Christian soul who joins our efforts. That soul is connected not only to us but also to the timeless people of God. When we serve and meet real human need through and within the congregation, we change the world, one situation at a time.

That's where the effectiveness of the congregation comes in. Few organizations know their neighborhoods and ministry areas as well as most congregations. If that knowledge can connect the service of Christian disciples within that church to those needs, there can be a rebirth of hope and vitality, care and compassion that is incredible. In fact, my friend joined and helped organize the effort to meet the needs of that family. And seeing how others in the congregation pitched in changed his perspective on the power of serving in the church.

A congregation I was affiliated with once served as a sponsor for a refugee family. When the family came, a house had been filled with furniture and appliances, casseroles and clothing. Members of the church had found work for the adults. With tears in their eyes, the parents stood before our congregation to simply say "thank you." For me it was a moving demonstration of the power of Christian serving in and through the congregation. The congregation literally changed the lives of one family. Because of the generosity of a group of Christians, they could begin again after having lost everything.

Questions for Reflection

❧ Have you ever been discouraged while serving in the church? What happened?

❧ On the other hand, have you ever seen the congregation rally to meet a critical need and be successful? What happened?

❧ How can service in the congregation really have the power to change the world for others?

❧ What are some ideas of how you might serve in your local church to really make a different world by meeting real needs in your community, our nation, or our world? Who would you invite to join you in this service?

IV. Bringing Justice into the Lives of Others

[God] has told you, O mortal, what is good; and what does the Lord require of you but to do justice, and to love kindness, and to walk humbly with your God?
　—Micah 6:8

Woe to you, scribes and Pharisees, hypocrites! For you tithe mint, dill, and cumin, and have neglected the weightier matters of the law: justice and mercy and faith.
　—Matthew 23:23

Make us worthy, Lord,
To serve our fellow men throughout the world
Who live in poverty and hunger;
Give them through our hands this day their daily bread
And by understanding love, give peace and joy.
     —Prayer attributed to Mahatma Gandhi

With malice toward none; with charity for all; with firmness in the right,
as God gives us to see the right, let us strive on to finish the work we
are in.
     —Abraham Lincoln

"What are you doing here, Pastor Mike?" he asked loudly. His face
was flushed and his voice was firm. "This is a complex issue and
the church has no business getting involved in it."

"I disagree," I calmly responded. "I fully recognize that the
issue is complicated. That's why we have affordable housing
advocates, rental unit and housing development owners as well
as city officials here. I believe that the church can, at the very
least, convene the conversation. This is the perfect time to do so,
with *Heart of the City* happening."

Burnsville, Minnesota, is a bedroom community to the Twin
Cities of Minneapolis and St. Paul. For decades it saw itself as
simply that—a community of neighborhoods overshadowed by
those metropolitan giants. Then, in the early 1990s a group of
citizens began a movement under the leadership of the mayor and
city manager to reinvent the city. *Heart of the City* became the
name for this effort for redevelopment. The vision was for the
first time to truly have a center to the city.

Prince of Peace became involved in this effort. At one point
we hosted a large meeting to discuss the urgent need for affordable housing in our area. It was, as you could guess from the

exchange set forth above, an effort that met with resistance from some.

On the other hand, it helped support and shape a marvelous outcome. As *Heart of the City* developed its plans and the city established necessary guidelines for redevelopment, the decision was made that 40 percent of the housing in that area would be dedicated as "affordable housing." More than that, rather than set the "affordable housing" off by itself, thereby creating a ghetto, it would be fully integrated. So a person couldn't tell from the outside if the town home was an upscale urban unit or one of the many "affordable housing" units. The effort was to cross not only lines of economy but also of social class.

Disciples of Jesus are, sooner or later, led into the public arena to seek justice for others. This can happen in a multitude of ways, but it usually grows in response to a particular need in a particular context. Disciples, by virtue of our calling, are leaders, and leaders exercise their faith within their context. From that particular context can emerge opportunities to participate in issues related to justice. The church may be involved in justice issues beyond the local level, but, as has often been quoted, "politics is always local."

Whether it is affordable housing, racism, sexism, or any of other "isms" that infect human community, creating unnatural barriers to the advancement of any person, the disciple of Jesus will be called to take a stand for justice in that place and time. The basis for this is at the core of our religion. We know that God sees "heart deep," not skin deep. God values every human being eternally, regardless of race, religion, social, political, or economic circumstances. Anything that compromises that conviction in the life of another human being weakens it within our souls.

The call for justice in the Bible is so repetitive that we can become deaf to its drumbeat! Like the conversation Jesus has so frequently about money, the continuing saga of God's demand for justice can be conveniently overlooked. But it is there, nonetheless, and our soul's value is tied to this will of God for justice.

In our time, when the engagement of the Christian in politics is so often met with suspicion, disciples of Jesus know that we are called into the public arena anyway. The question is not whether we are called there, but how shall we behave. The prophet Micah has given us clear guidelines: to *do justice . . . love kindness . . . walk humbly with God.* So we enter the sphere of political, social, and economic justice with the desire to *do something*—not just talk about it. But we do so with a heart of kindness and a bearing of humility. Biblically, I understand humility to be virtue of knowing who we are and who God is. It is a reverence for God and all that God values as well as a willingness to trust God with outcomes. The humble servant serves and then trusts that God will make of it something so much greater than even our greatest hopes and dreams. Those who oppose God's justice will eventually lose the battle and receive their judgment upon themselves. This is at the heart of that great passage quoted on page 88 from Lincoln's second inaugural address.

Doing justice is not an option for the disciple. The Mark of Discipleship called "service" requires mindfulness to what is just and good for both those within and those outside of the Christian church. The Mark of Service takes seriously that it is essential to the Christian church to live beyond itself. The church that lives to serve only its members has stopped being a church and become a club. The vision of God is for a people and an institution that changes the world for justice and good.

One of the great myths within the church is that those who are practicing personal piety will not be engaged in changing the world for good. We have heard it said, "She is so heavenly minded that she is no earthly good." I suppose that could be true in some cases. But the great workers for justice have often been motivated by a personal piety that moved them to do acts of kindness and work for justice. We need only think of Dr. Martin Luther King Jr. or Mother Teresa to make the connection between personal faith and justice. As people of the Savior, we called not only to tell about our faith; we are called to live our faith by working for the betterment of their lives and the community.

Questions for Reflection

❧ What issues of justice have called you into action?

❧ Have you participated in work for justice that changed your life, community, or world? What happened? Why or how did you get involved?

❧ Does the connection between personal faith and doing justice ring true for you?

❧ Who are some of your heroes of justice? How was faith a part of their courage and convictions?

CHAPTER 5

OUR CALL
TO RELATIONSHIP
WITH SPIRIT

THE MARK OF DISCIPLESHIP:
NURTURING RELATIONSHIPS

I. Family

Let marriage be held in honor by all.
—Hebrews 13:4

Children, obey your parents in the Lord, for this is right. . . . And (parents), do not provoke your children to anger, but bring them up in the discipline and instruction of the Lord.
—Ephesians 6:1, 4

Every child comes with the message that God is not discouraged of man.
—Rabindranath Tagore

The Christian home is the Master's workshop where the processes of character molding are silently, lovingly, faithfully and successfully carried on.
—Richard Monckton Milnes

We walked into the hospital room and were met by our daughter and son-in-law who were holding our new granddaughter, Emme. We had driven the three and one-half hours as soon as we received the phone call. Our daughter had previously lost three babies. Now, we joined them in the celebration of life and a healthy birth.

After Grandma took her turn holding Emme, it was my turn. I was awash with a flood of emotions as I sat down in the rocking chair. This birth was a true blue miracle! And a living miracle in one's arms connects to the deepest hopes in the human heart, hopes the Creator plants within each of us. Without thinking, I prayed for this little baby, my first grandchild. Then I took my thumb and made the sign of Jesus, the cross, on her forehead and whispered, "Emme Mikkel, you belong to Jesus and are marked with his cross in the name of the Father, Son, and Holy Spirit. Amen."

❧

The family is a gift from God and is intended to be that place where children receive the kind love and care that God wishes for all. Loving a child can be challenging. The first joy of a birth can be clouded by the fatigue of disturbed sleep. Night after night, a new parent is awakened to serve the needs of this new life. And as the child grows, his or her personality begins to emerge. Personalities are always a mixed blessing. There are parts of the self that are engaging and, often, inspiring. But the other side of an emerging self is the discovery of will. That's when the child begins to discover how to say, "No."

Family is not just the birthplace for individuals. It can be a forge for the formation of faith. Within the make-up of each child is the possibility of faith development and spirituality. But if these are not encouraged to grow, not brought to bear on the earliest self-expressions of the child, then faith can be lost—buried in the deep, dark places of undiscovered potential.

How can we rediscover the faith center of family? Disciples relate to those we love for spiritual growth, which means that we look for eternal lessons. Begin no matter what age the child is. First, pray for them, and pray for the lessons to be learned in life. Pray for God to both limit their pain and make the challenges of their lives spiritual lessons. Pray that the child will be held in the loving and care-filled arms of their heavenly Parent.

Second, remind yourself that parenting is a wonderful and yet difficult expression of "letting go" love. Parenting is the ultimate expression of loving and then giving away. Just as our God loved and brought to life our ancient ancestors, Adam and Eve, only to have them discover their emerging selves and flee his presence, so parents know that there will come a time when this beloved son or daughter will flee us. Our job is to prepare them for the best leaving possible. That includes preparing them in the faith. Life's journey can be difficult, but when the journey is undertaken with a faith perspective, the way is one of hope and the final destination is certain.

Third, pray with your child. Take the time to listen to concerns, hopes, and dreams. Then take those honestly to God with your child. Encourage your child to pray—to talk with God about anything and everything.

Fourth, read from the Bible to them and, as they grow older, read it with them. Help them understand that we can know the God to whom we pray. This wears the face of Jesus. Share with them that they will need to know this, because they will challenge and be challenged about who God really is.

Lastly, when the child is old enough to understand that they will eventually be on their own, speak to your child about their leaving. Tell them that you will support them in this natural process. You want it to be a good leaving so that they can return to you and the rest of the family again and again. Share with them that it will be hard for you, after all you have spent many years loving and "hanging-on." It might also be difficult for them as well. Think of the family as a launching pad for children's lives, not as a cage to keep them protected from the outside world.

The promise of this spiritual approach to parenting and family is the joy of their returning. That's part of what I experienced in that hospital room in Des Moines, Iowa. My daughter returned to me and brought a wonderful new life to my arms and heart. So now I pray for my children, the spouses they love, and the grandchildren I have been blessed with. I look to each separate life, each family, as an opportunity for me to both meet and speak of God. God has wonderful lessons to teach us through our children and grandchildren. The only question is whether we will be open to receiving them.

For example, we learn from our children and grandchildren that love returns to us. When we invest ourselves in them, the long-term return is our love, with interest. For example, here is a note we received from my daughter:

"I just wanted to thank you for the wonderful Christmas gifts and the time we spent. But more than all of that I just wanted you both to know how grateful I am that you are my parents. I can't tell you how blessed I am. No one could have been given a better mother or father. Love, Sarah"

When my wife and I read that note, our hearts were filled. We were grateful for our daughter's love—and for her selective memory. Isn't it true that, as parents or grandparents, we can get so caught up in the immediate situation that we forget that we're in it for the long haul? The payback for our love comes over time, and over that time God's hand blesses us with selective memory. This is, in most instances, a reflection of God's willingness to overlook our shortcomings and view us from the longest view possible—eternity. In a very real way, God teaches us about God's love in our family relationships. We also can learn the simple faith that gives birth to a great hope.

This past year, for example, my friend lost her husband of nearly fifty years. He had battled cancer valiantly and lost. He was a kind and generous man whose love for children and grandchildren overflowed at Christmastime. But this year, he was in heaven.

As my friend was leaving church one Sunday with her granddaughter, her granddaughter asked, "Does Grandpa have a Christmas tree in heaven? I hope he does."

"Oh, honey," my friend replied, "I'll bet he has the most beautiful Christmas tree you could imagine."

"Oh, good," her granddaughter sighed, "He'll have a wonderful Christmas too."

And of course, one of the greatest spiritual lessons we must learn in this life can be ours through family relationships. Everything in this life passes. Our children stay with us for a while and then they leave. Our grandchildren grow up and the close bond we feel with them thins out as they grow into their own lives. Everything we have—especially those things or persons that mean the most to us—is on loan from God. We are blessed to have them for the period we do, whether long or short.

God can come to us in our relationships with family, with children or grandchildren. The call of the disciple is to relate to them for the sake of spiritual growth—both theirs and ours.

Questions for Reflection

❧ What eternal truths have you learned from your children or grandchildren?

❧ Have you prayed for your children? Have you prayed with them? What happened in your relationship, if anything?

❧ Who nurtured you in the faith? If this nurture didn't come from family, where did it come from? Why is the family such an ideal place for such nurture to happen?

❧ If you have children or grandchildren, what prayers would you offer for them?

II. Meeting Christ in Our Friendships

The next day Jesus decided to go to Galilee. He found Philip and said to him, "Follow me." Now Philip was from Bethsaida, the city of Andrew and Peter. Philip found Nathanael and said to him, "We have found him about whom Moses in the law and also the prophets wrote, Jesus son of Joseph from Nazareth."
—John 1:43-45

When David had finished speaking to Saul, the soul of Jonathan was bound to the soul of David, and Jonathan loved him as his own soul.
—1 Samuel 18:1

You know who your friends are. They are the ones who take you out and buy you a cup of coffee the morning after your bankruptcy hits the paper.
—Bernie Wagnild

So long as we love, we serve; so long as others love us, I should say that we are almost indispensable; and no man is useless while he has a friend.
—Robert Louis Stevenson

"Well, pastor," he said with a grin, "I guess you're learning about mortality."

I didn't think it was funny. But my best friend was laughing as he said it. Having survived bouts of pneumonia, he knew the discomfort and slow recovery of the illness. But this was the first time I had ever experienced it.

Then he got serious. "You know," he said, "sooner or later we all have to face a struggle that is beyond us. This just happens to be yours this time. You've taught me a lot about faith. You know better than I do how God takes care of us. In the meantime, get some rest and take care of yourself. You're the best friend I've got."

There are few friendships like the ones where faith is shared. Mark became a Christian at Prince of Peace and was baptized a few years ago as an adult. His faith has grown, and so has our friendship. I suspect that there are very few things I wouldn't trust him with. His counsel and support have been invaluable to me personally. We have prayed together, talked about life together, and even huddled over ice fishing in the winter waters of Minnesota. I know that if something happened in my life that was tragic, he'd be the first person I would call. And I know that he'd drop everything and come. He knows the same about me.

So when I read about Philip and Nathanael, I get it. Great friendships are spiritual incubators. And I don't think true friends can keep their greatest joys from one another. Philip's great joy was meeting Jesus. He immediately wanted to share that joy with his friend Nathanael. If you love Jesus Christ and you love your best friend, you'll want the two of them to meet.

We don't make friends in order to get them to God. That's spiritual manipulation. But when we have a good friend, it is only natural that we would want to share the deepest parts of ourselves. Faith is certainly at the core of our being as disciples of Jesus. When it is the desire of our hearts, the conversation emerges naturally. I believe that Mark and I would be friends in any case. But I also know that sooner or later I would have had to talk about the Savior I follow and trust. If I weren't a Christian, I believe he would do the same.

Friendship is a spiritual trust from God. Close friendships are relationships within which we can learn of God's kind of loyalty. Without loyalty in friendship there is no love. And I believe that disciples of Jesus discover in him a loyalty that is nothing short of miraculous. In Jesus, God chose to set aside divinity in order to embrace our human condition. Jesus was loyal to God's love for us all the way to the cross. Love and loyalty in friendship exist together side by side.

That doesn't mean that real friends don't disagree with one another. It does mean that disagreement is placed within the context of forgiveness and a larger understanding and appreciation of the friend. That's what I think happened with David and Jonathan. When the Bible talks of their souls being bound to one another, it means that there was an appreciation and understanding of one another at the deepest level. If you know the story, you'll understand that their loyalty and love for each other survived the murderous treachery of King Saul, Jonathan's father—even overshadowing Jonathan's loyalty to his father.

Our close friendships built on a foundation of faith offer a glimpse of the eternal love of our heavenly Father. Such friendship grows deeper over time. I believe that Mark and I have a more comfortable and richer trust in one another as the years pass. And this too gives us a glimpse of the richness of God's friendship with us in Jesus. If my friendship with a man can grow that way, then I can only imagine what it will be like with God in eternity.

Friendship is also a gift of joy. Laughter comes easily with a good friend. I've often wondered if people could see that kind of friendship and trust in my relationship to Jesus Christ. My brother-in-law, Dan, taught me to enjoy prayer and even joke with God in prayer! Just as I think my friendship with Mark could not survive if I was always sober with him, so I enjoy laughing with Jesus Christ in prayer. It is a testimony, not to my brashness, but to my trust in the relationship God has given me in the power of the Holy Spirit.

Friendship has the remarkable possibility of growing our souls. The human spirit shrinks in isolation. I think that is why God made us for friendships with one another. Disciples of Jesus look for spiritual growth as a natural consequence of real friendship.

My friend Mark reminded me of that in the conversation recorded earlier. He reminded me that I am mortal, but he also told me that, between here and eternity, he was with me, concerned for me, and supported me. What a gift!

Questions for Reflection

❧ Whom do you consider best friend(s)? Is this friendship based on a shared faith in Christ?

❧ Have you shared your faith with your friends? Was it natural?

❧ How can friendship be an incubator for faith or a glimpse of heaven?

III. The Gift of Fellowship with Others in Small Groups

Six days later, Jesus took with him Peter and James and John, and led them up a high mountain apart, by themselves.
        —Mark 9:2

The next day he (Peter) got up and went with them, and some of the believers from Joppa accompanied him.
        —Acts 10:23b

He drew a circle that shut me out—
Heretic, rebel, a thing to flout.
But Love and I had the wit to win;
We drew a circle that took him in!
        —Edwin Markham

One of the most important phases of maturing is that of growth from self-centering to an understanding relationship to others. . . . A person is not mature until he has both an ability and a willingness to see himself as one among others and to do unto those others, as he would have them do to him.

—H. A. Overstreet

I got off the phone and was literally shaking. When I entered the living room where our friends had gathered for our small group meeting, Tom looked up and asked, "What's the matter, Mike?" I told them that it was our daughter on the phone. She was attending a college 2500 miles away at the time and she had just called, upset and scared. A man had pulled his car past her, and when she turned away he had called out to her swearing, turned the car around and began to chase after her. She had run through a park and found safety in the apartment of a friend.

I wanted to get on a plane and go be with her.

Rod looked up and said, "I think we should stop our conversation and pray for her safety right now." And the anger and fear began to dissipate as our friends began to surround our daughter with the very presence of the Holy Spirit.

The next day, she called back and was feeling much better. The school was on the lookout for the car and the man in it. She wasn't walking alone anymore. When I told her what our group had done, she said, "Thanks, Dad. It made a difference. I'll be okay. I just know it."

🜚

When Jesus went up on that mount for transfiguration he didn't go alone. He took a small group—Peter, James, and John—with him. This inner circle of close friends could wait with him, support him, and pray for him. Their relationship must have been remarkable, because on that fateful night of his betrayal, these three were with him in the Garden of Gethsemane.

Similarly, a small group of believers accompanied Peter when he was moved by a dream and by the voice of the Holy Spirit to break the kosher laws and travel with Gentile servants to Cornelius's house. They witnessed God's outpouring of the Holy Spirit on a Gentile household, and the doorway to God's promises blew open to a desperate world.

Throughout the centuries, Christians have gathered in large assemblies for worship and in small groups for spiritual growth and mutual support. In our time, we are discovering once again the power and joy of small groups.

Disciples of Jesus can find their lives of faith enhanced by gathering in small groups for personal sharing and caring. Small groups gather for a variety of reasons—to study and discuss the Bible, to pray for one another, and for the support of Christian love. I have found that certain steps are useful in forming a small group, such as the one that I describe—a group that mirrors Jesus and his disciples.

First, gather some people you like or would like to get to know. Make it clear that this is an opportunity for spiritual growth. Let them know that you want to reflect on faith and pray with and for one another.

Second, set the schedule for a given period up front. Be clear that the group is forming for a few weeks. This allows the participants to make a commitment for a specified time and it provides an easy out should anyone choose not to participate in the next round. I have seen people agree to continue in a group because they didn't want to hurt anyone's feelings or because they didn't know how to opt out. When the specified time is over, the leader can call each participant and, in the privacy of that phone call, discover how each person feels about continuing further as part of the group.

Third, set the ground rules. Confidentiality is a must. What is shared in the group stays in the group. No one, except the one sharing his or her story, has the right to talk to others about it. Should confidentiality be breached, the group disbands immediately.

Fourth, don't make the group meeting time a preparation burden. Since it is not a gourmet club, refreshments should be minimal. The host family should not have to feel obligated to prepare food for the group. The responsibility for leading devotions can be given to one leader, or it may be a task shared by different members of the group each week. Allow a person who is not comfortable leading to opt out.

Fifth, allow time for sharing personal news after the devotion. This is an essential way to help all to feel included in the group. Some people will feel more comfortable sharing personal news. Be careful not to let one person's news dominate on a regular basis. This is about mutual sharing. Listening is at least as important as talking.

Sixth, encourage each member to keep a prayer list. That way prayers requested by members of the group can be lifted up between meetings. And set the length of meeting time. The leader is responsible to keep the meeting within the time frame agreed upon. I recommend that ninety minutes be the time frame. The leader will need to interrupt and keep the meeting on track unless all the other members of the group overrule her.

Lastly, encourage consideration of a fun time apart from the group meeting for building the relationships, but let the group decide whether that will work with their schedules and interests. This is not a fellowship group. This is a group for honesty, support, and spiritual growth.

❧

"I had no idea how special these times would be," she said. "We both want the group to get together again. Would that be possible?"

I smiled. "Well, as a matter of fact, Chris and I had decided that we would be calling you and the other couples to ask if you wanted to participate in a prayer and growth group again or not. So we'll check in with the others and get back to you. But thanks for bringing it up. We need to connect again."

ৠ

Once you've experienced a discipleship group that works, you miss it when it is gone. That's what my friend was telling me. It matched what my wife and I were experiencing. It doesn't always work the first time through. Keep on trying; it will be worth it! Gather, pray, read the Bible, and share. Then watch what God's Spirit will do. We were created with a need for community, and a small group of believers is a wonderful gift to fulfill this need.

Questions for Reflection
ৠ Why did Jesus gather a small group of disciples?

ৠ If you have experienced the support and care of a small group of Christian disciples, describe what happened. If you haven't been involved in such a small group, would you be willing to try one?

ৠ What are the benefits of a group for spiritual growth?

ৠ Does your congregation have a program or organized small groups? If not, do you think you might be willing to help get one started?

IV. Sharing Jesus with Acquaintances

Always be ready to make your defense to anyone who demands from you an accounting for the hope that is in you; yet do it with gentleness and reverence.

—1 Peter 3:15b-16

But how are they to call on one in whom they have not believed? And how are they to believe in one of whom they have never heard? And how are they to hear without someone to proclaim him? And how are they to proclaim him unless they are sent?

—Romans 10:14-15a

Be like the bird
That, pausing in her flight
Awhile on boughs too slight,
Feels them give way
Beneath her yet sings,
Knowing that she hath wings.

—Victor Hugo

Most Christians really don't know what they have. If you have ever been outside the faith, apart from the church, you'll know what I mean. I have watched friends and relatives go through struggles and tragedies, joys and accomplishments without the privilege and joy of Christian community. My heart has broken for them, because I once left the faith and the church for a season.

While in college I became enamored of Buddhism. I remember setting my faith in Jesus Christ aside. My heart longed for God, and the expression of that longing became a seeking for God in reverie while walking by the rivers near my home out in the open country. But the God I sought had lost clarity and identity. The God of nature, the God of the wild-flower and eagle is also the God of the predator who strikes terror in the heart of the rabbit. The God of the dawn with all of its promise is also the God of the night when promise can slip into insomnia and hope can fade into bone numbing anxiety. There was no confidence or certainty.

Then one afternoon, while listening to music on my old stereo, Christ came slipping into my room. The Holy Spirit had transformed the yearning of my heart into a prayer, and I was surprised by joy. The crucified and risen One, like the prodigal's father, welcomed me back.

I returned to worship and then went to an adult Sunday school class led by a woman whose face I can still see. She invited me in and welcomed my questioning with a grace I still find remarkable. She and the other adults were so much older than this college student, but they were so willing to take time, to pray, and to listen.

That's when I discovered the church as a gathering of those who have been touched by the Spirit of Christ's love. Those who have never been outside of it, rarely have a clue about this treasure that we have been given. It is easy for us to overlook the best and see the worst. Still, the world is longing for the hope we have already received.

I think that Christians are sometimes unwilling to witness to the Savior because they have allowed evangelism to become no more than a set of questions about a person's eternal welfare. I will not argue with that, but the Christian joy we experience is more than salvation in the future. It is knowing Jesus and experiencing the fellowship of his people in the present. I returned to the church at the invitation of the Savior. I stayed at the invitation of some of his people. And I have never left.

Every human being longs for eternity. We give song to that longing when we invite others to know the Christ and his church. It's not about eloquence. It's not about eternal proclamations on the eternal consequences of unbelief. At least it isn't for me. It is a ready willingness to speak of the One who gives life with gentleness and reverence. I have discovered that there is a greater readiness to hear when a relationship has been built, which can form the fertile soil for the word of life. God's Spirit prepares the soil; my job is to "work the soil by simply sharing my story, telling of the One who stole into my room one day and reclaimed my life. In this way I can begin the process of bringing the receptive person into the community of believers.

The disciple of Jesus knows that sooner or later there will come an opportunity to speak in his name. We also know that we are not responsible for what others do with our words. We are responsible for how we share and in what manner we speak of him.

❦

"You are a pastor, aren't you?" she asked tentatively.

"Yes, I am," I replied.

"Will you please pray for my mother?" she asked.

"Of course, can you tell me a little about her needs?"

She began to tell me about the painful circumstances her mother was experiencing. When I asked this perfect stranger who had approached me in a coffee shop if I could pray for her mother by name, she thanked me, and I left that coffee shop. It was only in the parking lot that it dawned on me: I had missed a great ministry opportunity. No one was near us in that coffee shop, so I could have invited her to discreetly pray with me then and there. Even if she had said no, she would have had confidence that I really would pray for her mother. If she said yes, then the presence of the Savior would have been identified, for he was truly there. I resolved that next time that if I could do so without embarrassing anyone, I'd pray with the person then and there.

❦

Witnessing to Jesus is not hard, but it does require a spiritual readiness. The invitation to reveal the presence of God often comes from those who are seeking for comfort or strength or hope. Evangelism is telling the good news of God's love and loyalty, forgiveness, and grace to all humankind. It is not an intrusive declaration of judgment, and it is best shared by the one who has received the gift of that very love and claims the presence of Jesus at all times.

I once met Dr. Billy Graham. I was startled by his humility. I was taken by the plainness of his speech and the gentleness of his spirit. And that's when I got it. The power of his witness is in the character of his soul. But isn't that the way it is with all witnesses and all types of witnesses. Isn't it the one thing that Mother Teresa and Billy Graham have in common? No wonder they have touched the lives of so many. In them we meet the gentle reverence of a disciple.

My prayer is that others might see a similar presence in you and me.

Questions for Reflection

❧ If you have ever been separated from God what brought you back?

❧ How have you discovered the joy of being part of the church? What happened?

❧ Why do you think Christians are so often reticent to invite others to their church or to speak of Jesus in opportune moments?

❧ How are spiritual character and true witnessing connected?

❧ How do we prepare to give an accounting of the hope that is within us?

CHAPTER 6

GENEROSITY: A REFLECTION OF GOD'S HEART IN OUR LIVES

THE MARK OF DISCIPLESHIP: GIVING A TITHE AND BEYOND

I. Tithe

Will anyone rob God? Yet you are robbing me! But you say, "How are we robbing you?" In your tithes and offerings! You are cursed with a curse, for you are robbing me—the whole nation of you! Bring the full tithe into the storehouse, so that there may be food in my house, and thus put me to the test, says the Lord of hosts; see if I will not open the windows of heaven for you and pour down for you an overflowing blessing.
   —Malachi 3:8-10

Give and it will be given to you. A good measure, pressed down, shaken together, running over, will be put into your lap; for the measure you give will be the measure you get back.
   —Luke 6:38

We give Thee but Thine own,
Whate'er the gift may be;
All that we have is Thine alone,
A trust, O Lord, from Thee.
　　—William W. How

Blessed are those who can give without remembering and take without forgetting.
　　—Elizabeth Bibesco

"Mike, you don't tithe, do you?" Ted asked as we walked out of church after a council meeting. Ted was the church treasurer, and I had come to respect him over the three months or so that we had worked together. When I graduated from seminary there were three committees that Associate Pastors usually were assigned: Youth, Evangelism, and Stewardship. Ted and I worked on the Stewardship Committee together.

"No, Ted, I don't," I replied. "I don't believe in it."

"How can you not believe in tithing when the Bible teaches it?" he asked incredulously.

"I was never taught that it was biblical at seminary. In fact, I don't remember a single class on Christian stewardship," I responded.

"If I could show you that the Bible teaches tithing, would you do it?" he asked.

Well, I figured I had nothing to lose because I didn't believe tithing was biblical—at least not in the New Testament. So I agreed. After study and prayer, my wife and I became convinced that tithing was not only biblical but the assumption of Jesus. We looked at our giving, still among the top hundred or so in that congregation and found that we were giving at a 5-percent level, or half of a tithe. It took us four or five years to move to tithing, but we've done it since.

I believe one of the reasons that the witness of Christianity and the church is not stronger is because most Christians do not tithe. This is as much a spiritual deficiency as it is a financial deficiency. Tithing has nothing to with the church as an institution. It has everything to do with the heart of the disciple of Jesus.

God has provided us with everything we have, with who we are, and with what we are able to accomplish and acquire. God's people are simply asked to give one-tenth of their income in return. The tithe is not for God's sake. After all, God owns it all. The command to tithe is for our own benefit and for the benefit of others, many of whom have less. The allure of the things of this world is enormous. The treasures of this world are ours for enjoyment and betterment, but these things can very easily become the idols that own us. Tithing is a spiritual protection for our souls. And, as in every command of God, tithing is met with a promise.

The radical promise of the Savior is that we will receive, not just what we give, but "a good measure, pressed down, shaken together, running over." This corresponds to the promise in Malachi that God will "open the windows of heaven for you and pour down for you an overflowing blessing." In both instances the promise is simple: You can't outgive God.

Giving is an essential aspect of the life of discipleship. When the followers of Jesus become miserly, we turn from the best of ourselves. We have not been created simply to watch out for our own needs. When we claim God's gifts and hoard them for ourselves, we deny the destiny God has planted within us. Things that clutter our lives and our hearts keep us from discovering the joy of giving.

The example I like to give is holding onto an ice cube. The longer we hold it the smaller it gets as it melts. But take that ice cube and place it with others and it not only keeps its shape but can build and grow into an iceberg! When Christians give, God takes our giving and places it alongside the giving of others. Soon what seemed a small thing becomes a world-changing generosity. Only God can do this, but God invites us into a life-changing willingness to tithe.

The sixth Mark of Discipleship is Giving. This is the call to reflect the heart of God in our discipline of generosity. We have been created in the image of God. That means, in part, that every human being has within herself or himself a need to give. But sin, which separates us from God and clings to self, has turned our *giving spirit into an attitude of "gimme."* We turn to acquiring things, not realizing that we are turning from one of the essentials of joy and purpose. The truth is, getting more things does not translate into greater purpose and joy. We may have lives that are filled with things, but we may be spiritually empty.

The tithe is the foundation for our giving . . . not its ceiling. So how do we get there? First, let me suggest that you simply look at your take home pay. Then take one-tenth of that and you have a tithe. If your take home pay is $2,000 every two weeks, then your tithe is $200 every two weeks . . . and so on. If you are not tithing, it may be difficult to make that leap in one step. But push yourself to grow at least one percent of your take-home pay every year. Commit to grow to the tithe. And I encourage you to tell someone else that you are growing to a tithe in return for God's generosity.

Second, recognize that this is a lifetime commitment. You are making this an essential part of your financial stewardship plan. My experience is that tithers are among the best personal financial managers because tithing forces them to plan their personal budgeting. Such planning is, quite simply, good stewardship.

Third, I believe tithing is designed first to go to supporting the ministry of the church. The tithe does not include the extra giving of alms or the Old Testament practice of leaving the edges of the fields for the widows and orphans. In our time, charitable giving should first go to the church and then to the other organizations that serve as our "alms" or "gleaning" methods

Lastly, be prepared for the tithe to be both a source of temptation and great joy. It will be tempting at times to compromise your spiritual commitment. But look at it as an opportunity to grow strong in faith and heart. Your generosity will cause great joy, because you will tap into one of the least understood but most celebrated gifts of the human spirit—self-giving. This attribute is an essential building block for life purpose.

One more thing: please talk about tithing and giving with your children. Model your words by your actions. I have learned so much from parents who have made their regular giving as well as their additional charities a part of their family life. Their children have a spiritual head start in life that equips them for giving in a way that unlocks great personal joy.

Questions for Reflection

❧ Do you agree with the idea that the present weakness of the church is, in part, due to the lack of consistent generosity in its members? Why or why not?

❧ How does tithing fit into your commitment to Jesus? In what way is tithing a gift for the giver?

❧ What do you think of the idea that the need to give is part of the image of God within us? How have you experienced purpose through generosity?

❧ Do you agree or disagree that the tithe should go first to the local church? Why or why not?

II. The Power of Sacrificial Giving

A poor widow came and put in two small copper coins, which are worth a penny. Then he called his disciples and said to them, "Truly I tell you, this poor widow has put in more than all those who are contributing to the treasury. For all of them have contributed out of their abundance; but she out of her poverty has put in everything she had, all she had to live on."
—Mark 12:42-44

The point is this: the one who sows sparingly will also reap sparingly, and the one who sows bountifully will also reap bountifully.
—2 Corinthians 9:6

Love that is hoarded moulds at last
  Until we know some day
The only thing we ever have
  Is what we give away.
—Louis Ginsberg

To love is to know the sacrifices which eternity exacts from life.
—John Oliver Hobbes

Three boxes of food appeared on our doorstep. It was like the abundance of heaven had been poured down to us. The time was one of economic struggle for many. A billboard on the south side of Seattle, Washington, read: "Last one out turn off the lights." The economy in that region had collapsed. I was a student in college working for a United Methodist Church as a youth pastor, and my wife was a student working in a local day-care center. The church could not afford to pay my salary and the day-care center closed. We were without work and far from home. We had gone to the grocery store with the last $5 we had. When we returned, the boxes of food were waiting for us.

The members of the church, many of whom were out of work, had collected food for us. From their scarce supplies God provided abundance for the young couple they knew. It was a sacrificial gift that we have never forgotten, and it has stood as an ideal of sacrificial giving that we strive to live up to.

ᔑᒋ

Recently, our congregation was facing a financial crisis that was ultimately resolved through sacrificial giving. The biblical principle we grew to both understand and embrace is *equal sacrifice . . . not equal gift.* The point is that God has blessed some with more financial resources than others, but God has called all of us to experience the joy of sacrificial giving.

Sacrificial giving is not an end in itself. It is giving beyond the tithe for a great purpose. I don't know what great purpose moved that poor widow to give her last two cents to the church, but it must have been a great one. People who know the power of sacrificial giving have discovered that there are some things worth giving and living for. I suspect that was the motivation of that woman, and generations of Christians have been moved by her generosity ever since. We don't know her name, but we know her heart. It is her heart that the Savior praises.

The member of that Methodist congregation opened their hearts to my wife and me at time when resources were scarce. We were overwhelmed at the time, but now I think I understand much more deeply how God must have touched them. If you have never given in a sacrificial way, it is difficult to understand how that act shapes the human soul. What a great gift it is!

I believe this is what the apostle Paul is writing about in 2 Corinthians 9:6. He has experienced the power of sacrificial giving in himself. He is inviting the Corinthian Christians—and you and me—to experience it for ourselves. The outcome of sacrificial giving is a bounty of love and inner strength. Sacrificial giving is, I believe, a soul preparation for eternity.

Here's how to do it. First, find a cause that moves your heart. It must be a great cause through an organization that you trust. Second, give an amount above and beyond your regular tithing or offering that will change some of your habits or plans. One man I know gave up the specialty coffee he loves for a year and then multiplied the money he saved by two times and gave it to his great cause. A woman I know gave up her plans for remodeling her house and gave a large gift. Make it something that you can feel and see.

Third, make your gift with prayer. Surround the gift with your willingness to let go and trust that God will take it and multiply its effectiveness beyond your hopes. Then, every time you are reminded of the sacrificial gift, thank God for the opportunity and ask the Savior to lead you into a deeper willingness to see the abundance of God's blessings in your life.

Questions for Reflection

❦ Have you ever made a sacrificial gift? What was it for and what did you give up?

❦ What do you think of the concept of "equal sacrifice not equal gift"?

❦ What sacrificial gift might you consider giving now? What great cause would you choose, and what spiritual growth would you look for in yourself?

❦ In your experience, have you seen how God can take a small amount and do great work through it? Describe this experience.

III. Giving without Limits

For you know the generous act of our Lord Jesus Christ, that though he was rich, yet for your sakes he became poor, so that by his poverty you might become rich.

—2 Corinthians 8:9

Zacchaeus stood there and said to the Lord, "Look, half of my possessions, Lord, I will give to the poor; and if I have defrauded anyone of anything, I will pay back four times as much." Then Jesus said to him, "Today salvation has come to this house."
    —Luke 19:8-9

The world will never be won to Christ with what people can conveniently spare.
    —Bernard Edinger

Life truly lived is a risky business, and if one puts up too many fences against risk one ends by shutting out life itself.
    —Kenneth S. Davis

Mother Teresa was surprised. She had heard the family with eight children hadn't eaten in some time, so she took rice to the family. The mother of the family took the rice that Mother Teresa had brought into her hands and divided it in two. She took half of it and went out of the house and gave it to her neighbors. In explanation, she simply said, "They are hungry also."

What surprised Mother Teresa was not that this mother had divided her rice with her neighbors, she Hindu and they Muslim, but "I was very much surprised that she knew, because, as a rule when we are suffering, when we are in trouble, we have no time for others. Yet this mother knew and had the courage of her love to give" (*Reaching Out in Love*, Continuum, 2000, 32-33).

ᐁᖴ

Giving without limits is not limitless giving. We give from what we have, as the apostle Paul tells us, not from what we do not have. This wonderful story that Mother Teresa tells highlights this in a profound way. The woman's surprising gift gave expression to love in a surprising and simple way. She had so little, but she knew that her neighbor had less. So of her "little abundance" she shared what she had received.

Giving without limits is a risky business, but we have a Savior and Lord who doesn't ask of us anything that he hasn't already done. So when we think of giving without limits, we are to look to him. He sacrificed the wealth of divinity to become poor in his humanity. He gave his life so that we might inherit eternal life. From his sacrificial act come his power and his authority. He models the self-giving love that we are called to share.

Giving without limits is a way to really embrace of life—for ourselves and others. We have come to think of life as anything but a risky thing. We want to be safe. Even faith has been presented so often as a religion without cost. Zacchaeus, the sinner who had been touched by Jesus love, knew better. Who can hear his exclamation of generosity to Jesus and understand it as anything other than an exhilarating embrace of abundant life? He decided to give so generously in response to the wondrous embrace of God in Jesus Christ. Such an encounter with the living God always leads us to reach out to others.

Giving without limits witnesses to the world of the power of Jesus Christ to transform lives. As the church has tamed giving—making it an institutional need instead of the spiritual essential it is—we have also diminished the witness of the people of God. We have changed *giving from what we have* into *giving from our leftovers.* And the world watches. Still, I have seen and experienced a profound generosity from Christians.

❧❧

He approached me after the last worship of the morning. He had been seated in the front row, and I couldn't help but notice that this seven- or eight-year-old boy was remarkably attentive during the sermon on Christian giving. So when he approached, I stepped forward to meet him.

He took out his wallet and opened it, revealing three or four $1 bills. Then he said, "Pastor Mike, this is for the offering." He reached behind those ones and took out a $2 bill and gave it to me. I was touched, gave him a hug, and said thanks. Then I glanced at his waiting mother who was beaming. When she saw me looking at her, she simply winked. Her son, a modern day Zacchaeus.

❧

That little boy knew what he had. He knew where that $2 bill was—it was secreted away behind all those ones. But when he wanted to give, he gave without limits and reached right for that $2 bill! I have had the privilege, with the family's permission, to share that story with many others. It has been a wonderful testimony to the power of the gospel to touch and change lives toward generosity.

I have witnessed numerous times when God's people poured out gifts to meet a crisis in the lives of those they would never even meet. We held a special collection for the flood victims of a terrible devastation in northern Minnesota—and collected more than $60,000. When terrible earthquakes hit in India, we took another offering and received a similar amount! Giving without limits is beyond the tithe; it is the sacrificial gift for a great cause in response to a deep touch of the Holy Spirit. Most frequently it is in response to a critical need in the life of another. But sometimes, like that little boy, it comes in response to God having touched the soul's need to give more.

Questions for Reflection

❧ Describe a time when you have given without limits in an outburst of Christian gratitude? What happened?

❧ How can giving be seen as an opportunity to really embrace life?

❧ How are faith and giving risky when practiced in the manner Jesus describes?

❧ Do you think most Christians give from "what they have" or from "their leftovers"? Why?

IV. Money, Passion, Heart

Blessed are the merciful, for they will receive mercy.
   —Matthew 5:7

"I have no silver or gold, but what I have I give you; in the name of Jesus Christ of Nazareth, stand up and walk." And Peter took him by the right hand and raised him up.
   —Acts 3:6-7

Lord, you called to me,
And I did only answer thee
With words slow and sleepy:
"Wait a while! Wait a little!"
But while and while have no end,
And wait a little is a long road.
   —Anonymous

Good habits are not made on birthdays, nor Christian character at the New Year. The workshop of character is everyday life. The uneventful and commonplace hour is where the battle is lost or won.
   —Maltbie D. Babcock

The Salvation Army bell was ringing, but I was in a hurry. I had run late and needed to stop at the grocery store to pick up something for the evening meal. It was my turn to cook, and I had forgotten all about it until I was on the way home. So I looked down at the sidewalk and hurried by the old man standing in the cold ringing that bell.

Once inside the warmth of the store, I grabbed a basket and began my collection of food for supper. But the bell kept ringing, and with its noise in the background I couldn't help but picture that old man in the cold. I went to the "10 items or less" check out and was served quickly.

On the way out, I stopped to buy a coffee. Then, passing through the outer door, with the bell ringing even louder, I handed that cup of coffee to the old man and put a $5 bill in his bucket. For the first time since I remembered the meal I was committed to preparing, I felt an inner peace. In the cold and growing darkness I whistled "Hark the Herald Angels Sing."

§

The human heart is the playground of the Holy Spirit. The Spirit of God is constantly at work to invite us to joy, but often we are in such a hurry to be about the tasks in front of us that we cannot feel God's gentle touch. So the Spirit puts people and occasions in front of us. These are the "uneventful and commonplace" hours in which the formation of Christian character occurs. Each moment or encounter is an opportunity to connect the dots between money, passion, and heart; between giving and hoarding.

I have come to celebrate the fact that money can be the vehicle for accomplishing so much in our world. Oh, I don't mean that the little I give will eradicate poverty from our country, let alone the planet but I pray that someday we can do this by enlisting the giving of all who can afford to share. I know what stopping and putting a $5 bill in the Salvation Army kettle means for me: It is another opportunity to live what I say I believe. That's when money is transformed for me. That's when money becomes a spiritual commodity, and what it purchases is joy and strength for the soul.

Money and mercy go hand in hand. One is the gift; the other is the intent. When the gift is given, the intent is returned to the giver. The reality is that we truly cannot out-give God. So many of us have experienced the sweet touch of the Savior as we have stopped and given just that little extra. His mercy comes to us in greater quantity as we give it to others, doesn't it?

Recently we have launched an initiative at Prince of Peace we call Community Care Groups. These will be members and friends of the congregation who are in a limited geographic area. They will be our front line givers of mercy. When a need is identified, they will provide the immediate support. When a loved one dies, for example, they will provide the casserole and reach out in the name of Jesus Christ to provide loving support. Our prayer and intent is that this will be done for church members, but also for anyone else in the neighborhood. Whether the neighbor has a church or not, whether that neighbor ever worships at Prince of Peace or not, we want to be Christ's merciful presence in our community. This is the melding of our resources (money) with our Christian service (passion) and compassion (heart).

I have found myself dreaming of the quiet witness this might be—that our community would experience the care of God through the caring of God's people with no consideration given to a particular outcome in their response. We will do it because it is an expression of who we are, not of what we expect others to be or do. It could be a corporate expression of "putting five dollars in the kettle." We know that we will receive mercy as we extend it to others—even strangers.

Questions for Reflection

❧ Have you ever walked by a need only to have it bother you so much you returned and did more? What happened? How did you feel afterward?

❧ How is the human heart a playground for the Holy Spirit?

❧ Would you be willing to be a part of a neighborhood care group? What would you be willing to do? Who would you be willing to serve?

❧ How can the church transform your community? What would you be willing to give for it to do so?

V. Investing in Forever

Do not store up for yourselves treasures on earth, where moth and rust consume and where thieves break in and steal; but store up for yourselves treasures in heaven, where neither moth nor rust consumes and where thieves do not break in and steal. For where your treasure is, there your heart will be also.
—Matthew 6:19-21

How does God's love abide in anyone who has the world's goods and sees a brother or sister in need and yet refuses to help?
—1 John 3:17

Where has the Scripture made merit the rule or measure of charity?
—William Law

There are few moments when heaven's perspective intrudes into this world so clearly as when death nears. After nearly thirty years in the Christian ministry—six of them spent working with Hospice—I can testify to the power and grace of eternity's perspective. But I can also testify to the enormity of regret in the hearts of those whose lives had shrunk to selfish and self-centered limits, their charity limited to a grudging and infrequent giving.

Maybe that is why *A Christmas Carol* by Charles Dickens remains one of my favorite pieces of literature and performance. I believe that every day is an episode in our own *Christmas Carol*. Daily we are invited to the privilege of spiritual reflection on our relationship to Jesus Christ, and on our relationships with ourselves and others. Daily, the ghosts of Christmas past, present, and future tug at our hearts, not so that we would feel guilty but so that we might invest today in forever.

I am convinced that the only things we can take into eternity are the gifts of love we have given and received. The apostle Paul writes: "And now faith, hope and love abide, these three; and the greatest of these is love (1 Corinthians 13:13). Paul doesn't mean romantic love but rather the love that seeks expression in giving. This is the only aspect of our lives that lives into forever. Our faith will be fulfilled and our hope in Christ revealed, but love will grow. We grow this love whenever we see a brother or sister in need—and give.

She had been in the throws of dying for nearly eighteen hours. The family had kept vigil as best they could, and I had returned early the next morning. Finally, her husband, sitting beside her hospital bed and holding her hand, burst out, "Why doesn't God take her, Pastor Mike? Why won't God take her?" He fled the room sobbing. His daughter followed. I stepped around to that side of her bed and took the washcloth, dipped it in the cool water and began to wipe her brow.

In the silence—it happened.

Her son, a rebellious and distant child who had sat huddled in the corner as if to get as far away from her as possible, got up, took the washcloth from my hand and caressed his mother's brow. Then he bent over her, kissed her cheek and said, "I love you, Mom." She took a deep breath . . . and entered into forever accompanied by his love.

Charity is the giving of ourselves while holding nothing back. We experience heaven on earth in our expressions of charity. We dare to claim the promise of the Savior that such actions, such self-less giving, are truly investing in forever, storing up treasure where "neither moth nor rust consumes and thieves do not break in and steal."

We cannot grasp heaven, even in this life, and cling to the things of this world. I believe that dying woman was allowed to linger only until her son had let go of his anger and hurt and rebellion so that he could, with open hands, receive the spiritual gift she gave to him in that hospital room.

Pastors, hospice workers, volunteers, and many medical staff persons have seen and experienced what I did that morning. They know these are glimpses of eternity. They know that the things that make up heaven's perspective, that have an eternal value, are those things that cannot be measured by a price tag or brand logo. As followers of Jesus the Savior, we already know what has eternal value: It is the active self-giving love that reflects the love we have already received from our God. Anything less has no staying power and fades with the dawning of forever.

Practicing discipleship means investing our treasures where our hearts already are—in forever with Christ. We do this by responding to the opportunities to care for one another and others on this side of that great divide we call death. There is no such thing as miserly Christianity. We give a tithe and beyond in obedience to the commands of our God and reap a great harvest of joy. We will truly know that joy when we finally see our lives backward from heaven's threshold—surrounded by the love that we have given and received.

Questions for Reflection

❧ How is every day *A Christmas Carol* in your life?

❧ What do you think of the idea that active, giving love is an investment in forever? How is practicing our discipleship storing up treasures in heaven?

❧ How can we live so that joy, not regret, greets us on our deathbeds?

Some Final Thoughts and Questions

In this book's six chapters, we have covered some important and potentially life-changing questions. Take some time to consider all that has been read and possibly discussed. Then take some time to reflect on the following:

❧ As you think about the six Marks of Discipleship, name a couple of key new things you have learned.

❧ How has reading this book and working through its concepts changed you, or the way you think of the life of faith?

❧ For you, what is the meaning of the phrase "real faith for real life"?

❧ In what new ways do you sense God calling you to live or act or serve?

SIGNS OF SPIRITUAL GROWTH

❧ I find that I am able to trust God sooner in difficult circumstances.

❧ I find that I am able to accept God's forgiveness and let go of a wrong I have done earlier than before. ·

❧ I find that I am willing and able to forgive others more quickly and easily than before. Forgiveness is a three-step process:

First, I make the decision to forgive.

Second, I act *as if* the forgiveness has taken place.

Third, my feelings catch up to my decision and behavior.

This empowers me to learn about myself or the other and the action that caused my hurt.

❧ I accept failure more easily and learn from it.

❧ I can celebrate success and understand that it is ultimately a gift from God.

❧ I find that I am less inclined to try and control others.

❧ I am less judgmental of those who are different than me, or who have difficulties I cannot understand.

❧ I find that my anger has more to do with the wrongs done to others than to my own will.

❧ I find that I am speaking and listening to God throughout the day.

❧ When I awake in the middle of the night, the first question I ask is what or whom God would have me pray for.

❧ I am more frequently and freely generous with my resources—especially my money.

❧ I have discovered the difference between happiness and joy.

❧ My life is grounded in purpose.

❧ I trust that my value as a person has already been established in God's love for me.

❧ I find that I look for blessings more often—and I see them.

❧ I delight in children and see youth in the eyes of the aged.

❧ My life's priorities are clear: God, family, friends, and then self.

❧ I am committed to self-care and respectful of the self-care of others.

❧ I experience joy in the success of others.

❧ God speaks to me through the Bible.

❧ I see worship as an opportunity to be with God in the midst of God's people.

❧ I have a group of friends with whom I can be spiritually honest and real.

❧ I experience joy in simple acts of service and kindness.

❧ My heart is lifted when I sing or hear songs of praise to God.

❧ Prayer is my first response to real human need.

Other Resources
from Augsburg Books

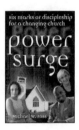

Power Surge by Michael W. Foss
184 pages, 0-8006-3264-8

Foss makes the case for transforming congregations
from a membership model to a discipleship model
of church affiliation. Provides practical helps for
assessing the present and strategies for moving
into the future.

A Servant's Manual by Michael W. Foss
144 pages, 0-8006-3453-5

Foss traces the larger cultural shifts that affect the
church's position in the world and styles of leadership. He then diagnoses church thinking as largely
reproductive of past successes and ineffective in this
new context.

Let the Servant Church Arise! by Barbara DeGrote-
Sorensen and David Allen Sorensen
96 pages, 0-8066-4995-X

Explores all aspect of Christian servanthood and how
it can have a profound effect on both church and civil
communities. Encourages readers to discover purpose
and meaning in life through serving others.

Available wherever books are sold.